Nine Tana Leaves

Nine Tana Leaves

James Noble

ISBN: 0692993304
ISBN-13: 9780692993309

Dedication

For my whip-smart, creative son and daughter,
Oliver and Rebecca, who inspire me every day.

For my wonderful wife, Cheryl, who worked so hard on this book and is as loving and beautiful a wife as one could ever hope for. I love you.

And especially to Katharina Grunberg.

Acknowledgments

I WOULD LIKE TO THANK the true friends and family who have stuck by me through thick and thin. I am indeed a lucky man. My mom and dad; Scott and Donna Sheinberg; Peter Green; Matt Smith; Kevin Morse; Tom Schaefer; Ed and Patsy Van Eck; Darryl Rubscha; and my brothers, John and Scott Noble, who pushed me to write this book.

Contents

Growing old is mandatory; growing up is optional.

— Chili Davis

Much of what happens in here really happened.

Street of Dreams

THERE ARE GHOSTS ON WEST Ambler Road—not specters of fear like Jacob Marley, but just the same, these are apparitions of what once was. As I drive down my old road, Mr. Biser, dead for twenty years now, mows his lawn with a scowl that would melt ice cream. In the upstairs window of the Hirlington place, my ten-year-old pal wears *Lost in Space* pajamas and waves. I can see his trademark *I'm-grounded-again* face. My canine nemesis, Duke, is barking up spittle and chasing my car, as he did so many times to Dad's Impala. That old bat Mrs. Munson is gardening. Our tree fortress is still clumsily nailed to the giant oak in the meadow.

And at the end of the cul-de-sac stands the three-bedroom ranch house I inhabited for the first eleven years of my life. It's a different color now, a little worn, and a lot smaller than I remember it being in 1972. And yet it's still larger than life. The front lawn is cut, neat, and manicured. The bushes we would land on after jumping from the roof are no longer there. Our meeting place, the fence post, is gone, replaced by one of those elaborate playground sets.

I pull to the side of the road and park. Next to me, in the passenger seat, is a battery-operated record player from Japan I found at a yard sale. Miraculously, it's similar to the one my brother and I shared thirty years ago. Like a forensic scientist handling evidence, I remove a golden-oldie record from a leather case on the floor. I place the single on the turntable. As I turn the player on, the needle sinks into the first groove of the vinyl. No scratches. My eyes close slowly, as if I'm being anesthetized. I envision it all.

The Schwinn bicycle jump of death. The evil neighbors. The deadly swarm of bees. The girl who ran away with my soul. The woman who changed my life. Deeper into yesterday I fall.

And then Looking Glass begins to sing "Brandy."

The Myth of Jimmy Foxton

Early in the spring of 1972, my seven-year-old brother Jeremy and I came home from an evening of chest pains and pummeled dreams, otherwise known as Little League tryouts.

This dreaded annual event offered unknown men the chance to rate your cherished baseball skills with the sensitivity of a vending machine. As always, cutting through the Belfasts' yard was our preferred route. This particular evening we decided to take the shorter and far ballsier trek through the Munsons' backyard, a sprawling botanical nightmare littered with life-size plastic deer and Buddha statues with empty eye sockets and hideous grins. As Jeremy and I speed walked past the ornate graves honoring the Munsons' former dogs, we heard Mrs. Munson laugh.

She always cleared her wrinkly white throat with an unmistakable "Hmmpprrh," and we were used to her bellowing out to the street, "You boys take that baseball game elsewhere, or I'm letting out Duke! Hmmpprrh."

But nobody was scared of Duke, her sixteen-year-old border collie, who was days away from being taxidermied and buried in the backyard himself.

I turned and gave my brother the hand signal to follow me into danger. The inhabitants of the woods chirped and clicked in eight-track quadraphonic sound. Jeremy crouched behind me as we desperately tried to step on as few branches as possible. Bright lights from the house lit up the unsettled pool waters and bounced directly into our eyes.

Squinting, we barely made out the surroundings. But it was just enough, for suddenly before us stood a terrifying spectacle to rival any horror movie.

The great mystery of the feminine body was unveiled with the grace of an uppercut to the jaw. Sixty-five-year-old Mrs. Munson was naked. She attempted to daintily climb the diving board while her giantess figure almost snapped the wooden plank in half. She grabbed her nostrils and disappeared in a thunderous splash. Mr. Munson, also naked, climbed the board. Jeremy broke our sacred code of silence with an "Ewwwwww" that emanated deeply from his diaphragm. There was a moment of eerie quiet, followed by some whispers.

Then the lights went out.

We could hear the metallic screeching of chaise lounges being moved around the patio. On our bellies we inched near enough to smell cigarette smoke and taste the chlorine in the backs of our throats. The giggling continued, and ever so quietly we got to our feet and peered over the fence. Of course my memory has long since been eroded with this trauma, but I'm pretty sure Mr. Munson was atop Mrs. Munson, giving her a hickey. She was laughing.

She was making her *Hmmpprrh* sound. I had never seen so much skin. I had never seen so much skin covered with so much hair. I can really only describe what I saw with three words: *Oh*, *God*, and *No*.

Jeremy was already running. I stood and staggered backward, dry heaving and gagging. I turned and tripped over a plaster mushroom. I got up quickly and bolted. The rhythm of crickets now sounded as if they were collectively laughing at me. Every passing tree seemed to have a twig for my hair. This was Snow White's dark forest.

Then my foot caught another mushroom…except it wasn't a mushroom. It was Duke, sleeping on the grass. I fell down upon the recently watered lawn and slid fifteen feet. Duke bumbled toward me. As blood ran down my leg, the dog broke out in a toothless howl.

"Shh, Duke. Shh, Dukey. Dukey," I begged.

"Duke! Duke! You find something, my little sweetie? Hmmpprrh," howled Mrs. Munson.

I froze and looked for an escape route, but the lawn was too long and too wide.

The only place to hide was a large bush ten feet back up the slope. I crawled and burrowed into the foliage. Duke was now in full-on barking mode.

Mrs. Munson repeated, "Dukesy. Dukesy. Mama's comin'."

Duke easily found me in the bushes as I wedged myself under the largest branches. As he sniffed and scratched, I saw an enormous pair of bleach-white ankles walking my way. If I got caught, it would probably mean a spanking and two weeks grounded in my room; however, the upside would be legend: the grand tale of ten-year-old Jimmy Foxton crashing an X-rated pool party would travel from here to Fairfield. Of course Duke had another idea, and that was to bite me. His toothless jowls snapped inches from my nose.

Mrs. Munson arrived panting, naked, and screaming for her husband to bring a pellet gun. Mr. Munson came running and grabbed Mrs. Munson from behind. As Mrs. Munson babbled about a raccoon in the bushes, they both fell to the ground. Mr. Munson was groping Mrs. Munson's huge bosom. Duke kept trying to bite me, and Mrs. Munson kept ordering the dog to keep quiet.

By this time I thought Jeremy might be getting worried or—worse—telling Dad. I looked at the gash on my leg and wondered how I would explain all this to my mom. I gazed back up at the whalelike orgy, and Mrs. Munson and I locked eyes. I don't know who was more shocked. She stopped giggling, and her lips pulled back to reveal those white chompers.

Mr. Munson also turned toward me, and I noticed that he *wasn't* Mr. Munson. It was Mr. Biser from down the street. He got up, white-faced and white-assed. He ran into the moonlight like we were at the end of a Laurel and Hardy movie. Mrs. Munson didn't say a word as she rose. She grabbed Duke by the collar, and the ole boy yelped something good. I got to my feet, and there we were—Holmes and Moriarty, sizing each other up with steely eyes.

A minute that seemed like forever passed. She raised her hand, and that crooked finger pointed me off the property. I did not look back.

My mother and father never found out what happened. Jeremy never stopped inquiring about the incident, as if his repeated grillings would garner more details.

But Mrs. Munson and Mr. Biser would not forget. I had wrought my very first enemies, and they were formidable ones too. The rest of that summer, I felt their predatory eyes on me.

And one day they would strike.

Where Eagles Dare

In fifth grade, I wrote an essay entitled "Who Am I in 100 Words or Less." It began awesomely:

> My names is James Richard Foxton. I am ten years old. I have black hair, green eyes, mom says a "pleasant smile" and I like monster movies. The color ones where Dracula speaks like James Bond. And the black and white ones too on Creature Features every Saturday night like Fiend Without A Face. You should see it! When I grow up I want to make monster movies. I have a mom and a dad and a brother. My dad makes ads in New York and Mom makes good pizza. I have two best friends. Shilling and Hurl.

It was only ninety-nine words, but it summed me up quite well. As for my two best friends, they deserve a far better explanation.

Hurl was a little taller than the rest of us—a giraffe type—and the only one allowed to grow his hair longer. His parents were closet hippies and always playing "that racket," as my dad referred to the Allman Brothers and Pink Floyd. The music would drift from their open windows into the summer nights. Hurl's real name was Hirlington, but Shilling had dubbed him Hurl for his infamous stunt on Where Eagles Dare, the tree fort that served as our refuge from a planet we didn't yet understand or want to.

Hurl's house was the only property that looked like it didn't belong on West Ambler Road. Once upon a time, it probably had been a nice-looking little cottage. Now it was a shack. The front yard was overgrown with straggly bushes that housed several large and mean wasp colonies. The grass was yellow, spotty, and sprinkled with an occasional lush patch of olive-colored weeds that grew as tall as a stalk of corn. Every time we drove by his house, my dad would mutter, "How could a family live in a cesspool like that?" I had no idea what a cesspool was, but from his tone, I knew it wasn't good.

The house smelled something awful. The second you crossed the invisible border from the asphalt street onto Hurl's jungle of a lawn, you could detect a staleness—a touch of moldy closet with a hint of rotten egg. It was bad enough to make me squinch my nose every time I visited. We never played in the Hirlingtons' yard.

Hurl's dad was a hunchbacked guy who owned an old-fashioned pharmacy that was being threatened by "those damn little convenience stores everywhere," Mr. Hirlington would say. Usually he said things like this on the weekends, when he was drinking beer. Hurl's dad was the oldest of all our parents, and like his house, he didn't fit in on our street. My dad would wave to him, but I never saw them have a Coke or watch football together, like Dad did with Mr. Shilling. As I saw it, Mr. Hirlington behaved more like a grandpa than a pa.

Hurl's mom was called Francine…but only by Mr. Hirlington. Everyone else called her Franny. All Franny's friends would come over to play cards and drink cocktails on weekday afternoons. That meant the first thing that happened when you entered Hurl's house after school was that you'd smell the stink of dry, itchy-throat smoke mixed with a whiff of alcohol. It reeked like the science lab in school—only worse. Sometimes it was so thick I had to hold my breath until I got up the stairs and into Hurl's room.

Hurl was an enigma. He'd spout the wisdom of an adult, yet he had H.R. Pufnstuf posters on his wall. He also had trolls, a girlie thing I never understood and never asked him about.

Once in his room, you couldn't help but gaze out his window to his forlorn backyard, which was worse than the front yard. A forbidden place littered with rusted patio furniture turned upside down, a moss-covered brick deck, and an old grill overrun with black soot, it was gross. And haunted not with monsters but with memories of picnics, badminton games, and swell times we'd had before the Hirlingtons moved in—back when the Tysons had lived there. I had been just a baby, but I do remember cookouts, inflatable pools, and horseshoe games.

Hurl was a year older than our classmates. He'd been held back in first grade because Mr. Tardney had thought he was slow. For a fifth grader, he was a lumbering giant of a boy, not big or beefy but an Ichabod Crane type who wore clothes that were too small and childish. The kids at school called him Barkers after the secondhand clothing store downtown where his mom purchased his shirts and pants.

When it came to school-yard kickball, however, it was all a different story. Hurl was always picked first; his long, sinewy legs guaranteed a home run almost every time. He was a complete goof until he stepped onto the baseball diamond.

Like Franny's, Hurl's hair was a jet-black mop. And also like Franny, Hurl always appeared sad, even when he was laughing. He sat directly behind me in homeroom, and I didn't speak to him for two years. When the school bus dropped us off at the foot of West Ambler Road, none of us said squat to him. It was cruel, mean, and what kids do to one another.

One day we exited the bus and began the ascent up the first hill of our street. Behind us Hurl began filling his pockets with rocks. We turned to look at him gathering stones, and Shilling made a "he's crazy" face.

At the top of the hill, we passed our best climbing tree, which we'd named Where Eagles Dare after a movie we'd seen at the Nugget Theatre the previous fall. Where Eagles Dare was a humongous oak tree. Its natural design was perfectly suited for boys. And adventure. The trunk was ten feet in diameter, and the first branch was only four feet off the ground. We used an old milk crate to help us climb those first glorious feet and take us into the sky.

Heading up the tree, we would first come to Machine Gun Peak, a ramshackle collection of plywood boards screwed to a branch forty-five feet off the ground. It was just big enough to accommodate the three of us at one time. We had meetings up there—serious discussions like who was going to chair the committee to organize the egging of the Munsons' house or how we would fund the ongoing drive to buy an equally shared minibike.

Way above Machine Gun peak was Crow's Nest. Eighty feet off the ground, Crow's Nest was a single two-by-four hammered in with three one-inch nails. It was so flimsy it would hold only one of us. Just a minor slip and you'd be toast…or, better yet, scrambled eggs on the ground below.

Suddenly Hurl bolted toward Where Eagles Dare and began climbing it faster than anyone we had ever seen. It was pure brutality and grace. His orangutan feet moved with subtlety, while his hands betrayed his awkwardness and snapped every branch he touched. We curiously watched for a brief second, then shook our heads and walked homeward.

Later that night, as I was manipulating my brother into trading a Willie Mays baseball card for an unknown right fielder for the Cubs, Mom walked in on the grift and asked if we had seen "that Hirlington boy. His mother called."

I blurted out, "He was climbing Where Eagles Dare last time we saw him."

And that was the end of it until Dad came home an hour later. (Our father was the only man I have ever seen who could take off his jacket, loosen his tie, read the paper, and make a martini at his wet bar at the same time. Once Jeremy and I clocked it at one minute and thirty-six seconds from when the front door opened to when he sat on the couch with a cocktail.) He mumbled something about a fire truck and a police car parked underneath "that big tree you boys climb."

I looked at Mom, who looked at Jeremy. We immediately got up and went to the door. I imagine Dad just sat there, quite glad he could drink and read in peace.

Jeremy and I ran down the lane in darkness—we could have navigated it blindfolded. The blinking lights of the emergency vehicles came out of nowhere. The Shillings, Mrs. Munson, and even Mr. Biser were all gathered below the giant oak. They were all looking straight up, crooking their necks.

"The Hirlington kid flipped his wig," Mr. Shilling announced as we arrived.

Over near the fire truck, I saw Hurl's mom and dad talking to the fire chief. Franny was wiping a tissue over her eyes, but I didn't see any tears. Mr. Hirlington, on the other hand, looked sweaty and exasperated. He was gesturing wildly and pointing upward. Then I saw a fireman put on his helmet and head up Where Eagles Dare.

The second his foot touched the first branch, down came the rocks at full speed. One hit the fireman in the helmet with a loud clank. Another big one cracked him square in the shoulder, and he groaned. He stepped back down and walked over to the Hirlingtons, who continued to throw their arms in the air.

More people came, and this started to look like it would be front-page news on the playground the next morning. The people standing by seemed to have made up their minds already that the Hirlingtons were terrible parents. They shook their heads.

I don't know exactly why, and I don't know exactly how, but I started to walk toward Where Eagles Dare. I heard Mom deliver a stern "James Foxton" to the back of my head, but I kept on. I was making my way under the low-hanging branches when I yelled up, "Hey, Hirlington. It's me, Jimmy Foxton."

Silence.

"Can I climb up? Never done it at night," I said in my best don't-throw-rocks-at-me voice.

Nothing.

I looked at the crowd, who were now speechless and put my foot on the first branch, fully expecting to get beaned. A slight rustling came from above but no rocks. I ventured farther upward. Looking down, Mr. Hirlington give me a nod of encouragement. His eyes were filling with tears of uncertainty… and maybe a little hope. I turned my attention to the dark forest above and went on. My leg slipped once, and there was a collective gasp just like the theater audience had made when Richard Burton climbed the cable car in the movie the tree was named after.

Hurl wasn't at Machine Gun Peak. He was on the Crow's Nest. We looked at each other and said nothing. We didn't need to. He was gonna jump.

If I didn't want kid splatter all over the street, I knew I'd better do what no kid had ever done: join Hurl on that shaky two-by-four. When I got up there, sweaty and out of breath, Hurl was looking out over our town. It dawned on me that I really had never been this high at night before. My eyes opened wide, and for the briefest moment, I forgot about our situation. The whole spectacle of the town below us resembled a tiny train set. All those lights. All those roads leading to who knew where. The temporary spell was broken by the fireman way, way below us, who yelled up, "You OK, son?"

"Yeah," I hollered back.

I looked at Hurl. "Hey," I muttered.

"What are you doing here, Foxton?" he half snarled.

"You can call me Jim."

Hirlington threw one of his stashed rocks into the night.

I took another chance. "What are you doing up here? Your dad's having a connipshit."

"Yeah, well, my mom's leaving me and my dad and going to live in Fairfield," he said.

I let this sink in for a moment. Our street and us kids had been luckily spared the horrors of divorce so far. Sure, there was trouble in some houses—Mr. Biser had lost his job, and his wife had died of some disease we couldn't pronounce years ago—but no household had ever ventured into family-breakup territory. I knew of divorce from TV shows, but I'd never thought it would happen here. I didn't know what to say. But Hurl did.

"They told me last night. First my mom comes in all sad and stuff and starts telling me it's for the best. That her and Dad were not happy and that I should want my parents to be happy," he said, whimpering so low I could barely hear.

"Then my dad comes in and sits on my floor, and he starts to cry. Like, really cry. At first I thought he had punched a wall. Maybe hurt his hand or something. He tells me that my mom had met some other man who made her more happy. So he had to let her go. He said if you love something more than anything else in the world and let it go, it will come back. And then he just started crying more. Like a baby." Hurl was spitting the words as his eyes got red, just like his dad's did sometimes after drinking too much.

"Hirlington…geez. I don't know what to say." Obviously my well of wisdom had run dry. It didn't matter. I didn't think he'd even heard me.

He continued, "It's like one day you're fine. The next everything is gone… you know what I mean? Everything is just…gone."

I nodded, having no clue what he meant. I just kept looking at him and trying to be anything he wanted so he wouldn't take the leap.

He was now at a full-blown crying stage. "This morning my mom tells me I'm going to have a new father and a new baby brother, and I should be really excited. I already hate it. And I hate her. I didn't know what to do except come up here where nobody can bother me." His mouth was covered in snot dripping from his nose.

He continued, mucus and all, "Thought about jumping, but it looked like it would hurt."

Hirlington looked at me and laughed. I started to laugh too. I held my hand out for a rock, and Hirlington handed me a doozy. I flung it into the night, and we waited. Then came the triumphant sound of clanging metal. *Hole in one*, I thought.

"I'm not boring you, am I?" I said.

"Nah, you're cool. I always liked you, even though we never talked."

I didn't know what to say to that either.

Hurl added, "We should partner up in biology sometime. I think we're gonna cut up a tadpole soon."

This was a fact. Shilling and I were already expecting to ace the test in amphibian anatomy—we had been blowing up things in Bales Pond for ages.

"Too bad we can't use black cats," I said, referencing our preferred firepower.

"Oh man, last week I blew up a Matchbox car with an M-80," Hirlington said proudly.

He immediately impressed me to no end. Every once in a while, I could get my hands on a piece of thunder like a cherry bomb…but an M-80? There was nothing more coveted on the kid black market. We had heard stories about their power, and once we saw the tough kids on the other side of Ambler Road blowing up plastic models with them, but none of us had ever held such a piece of weaponry.

"You got any more?" I asked hopefully.

"I have a footlocker full of them. My cousin from Ohio brings them all the time. In Ohio you can buy them at the grocery store."

"Whoa," I said. It was the only thing I could say to such wonderment.

"You wanna light some off Saturday?"

"Yeah. Can Shilling and my brother, Jeremy, come?"

Hirlington looked a little perplexed. "I don't think those guys like me. And I'm not sure I like them either."

"Ah, Shilling's cool. My brother's a wad. No problem. You'll like them."

I finally found the gumption to move closer to Hurl. I slid over on the thin piece of wood, and my butt suddenly felt air. I was falling.

I grappled for a hold on a lower branch, but it was too thick, and I couldn't get my hands around it. My head slammed into the tree, and everything started to spin. Just as I started getting that roller-coaster feeling in my belly, my neck tightened as if in a noose. Gagging and barely able to breathe, I twirled in the wind like a hanged man. I stared into the darkness, dumbfounded and numb. Slowly I looked upward. Hirlington was grimacing as he held the back of my hooded sweatshirt.

My shirt was raised so high that my bare stomach rubbed against the barbed-wire bark of Where Eagles Dare. I was bleeding pretty badly. Hirlington was a big kid but not necessarily a strong one. Even in the dark, I could see his face turning a different color. I could hear him grunting and groaning. It sounded like he was saying, "Graaaaab the braaaaaaancccccchhhhh."

I wasn't asleep, but I wasn't awake either. It felt a little like when I'd had my molars out, and the dentist had given me gas.

"Foooooxtooon." Hirlington was really bawling now. "Graaaaab the braaaaancccch! I caaaaan't..."

I was dangling in the air eighty feet up on Where Eagles Dare.

My brain finally began to generate thoughts, and I didn't care about the pain anymore. I grabbed the trunk with all my might and straddled it with my legs.

"You got it?" Hirlington said.

I nodded and immediately felt the air coming back into my lungs. Then I started to weep too.

Hirlington reached for my hand to try to pull me up, but I wasn't ready. I held on to that trunk for life.

Little by little, my Converse All Stars grabbed hold of the tree and inched me upward. My hands slowly released their death grip on the bark, and I found the strength to pull my bloody torso topside.

Hurl reached for the back of my bell-bottoms and yanked me up. I huddled on the main branch facedown. Now I was bawling from the shock and from the pain.

We sat there for another fifteen minutes, not saying a word. Hirlington grabbed his bandanna from his coat pocket and handed it to me. I wiped the blood from my belly and all the sweat and grime from my face.

Down below us I heard yelling. Everyone was probably still gazing up and judging Mr. and Mrs. Hirlington. Maybe even Hirlington knew that. He was about to commit an act that would define him forever.

We were both catching our breath when I heard the first gurgle. Hirlington was turning green. I guess all the muscle work, stress, and panic had really gotten to him. He looked over the edge and yacked more throw up than I had ever seen in my life. It must have been pounds of chunks and yellow liquid and spit. Honestly, I don't know how we managed to not fall off with such violent convulsions.

Mr. Peterson felt it first—a small droplet on the back of his balding head. *Rain?* he probably thought.

Then Mrs. Munson got a dab on her cheek. She wiped it away with her gloved finger. *Seems a little heavy for water*, she probably thought. She looked at her pinkie and seemed confused by the thick, gooey, colored spot with slime-like consistency.

Then it came down. Hard. On everybody. A continuous stream of liquefied meatloaf, mashed potatoes, mushy peas, and Hawaiian Punch.

The mob under Where Eagles Dare dispersed in every direction. Some were lucky, and some had a vomit shampoo. One thing was for sure: everybody knew we were still alive way up there.

After Hurl's five-minute projectile demonstration, we both knew it was time to get down. He nodded, and I finally smiled.

"Don't tell anyone I cried," he said nervously as he wiped his chin.

"Don't tell anyone *I* cried," I said and chuckled.

Below we heard the fireman scream again, and we hollered that we were coming.

I was sore, but there was nothing that could keep me up on Where Eagles Dare any longer.

Hurl, as he was now known, went down first. When he finally stepped onto the milk carton, his parents grabbed him and hugged him, and I imagined that felt pretty good. I saw my mom and dad looking up, their facial muscles relaxing as they watched me stagger off the tree. Proud of me, my mom assaulted me first, squeezing my concealed wounds so hard I could have upchucked myself. But I held it in.

The crowd now bunched around us. Random people gave me high fives, and other dads congratulated my dad. I looked around for Jeremy, but he'd been pushed out by the older guys. Then, amid all the shadows and movement, I saw his petrified face. We connected for a moment, and I winked. His face broke into a full-fledged grin, and he mouthed the words *ass face.*

From the corner of my eye, I saw Hurl being led off by his parents, a blanket draped around his shoulders. He looked back at me, expressionless. We both knew he was going back someplace dark.

But we also knew that now we would face it together.

The Telltale Toro

For the rest of that sticky summer, my two best friends, Jeremy, and I gathered around the fence post that divided our homes. It was hardly unusual, considering we'd spent all the summers before at that very same location. The four of us knew nothing of other streets or other towns—as far as we were concerned, the world and all its problems lay on that half mile of asphalt known as West Ambler Road.

In the evenings, when garage doors were left open, the soft yellow glow of sixty-watt bulbs and dancing moths would put on glorious and creepy shadow-puppet shows. The fireflies would be out, and our jars were ready. The four of us pranced around the yard with our jars held high, just waiting for that hovering spark to show itself. After fishing for fireflies, we'd put all our jars atop the fence post and stand back. The jars would light up like instruments in Frankenstein's laboratory, and you could see the glow two houses down. Shilling's jar would go off. Then mine. Then Hurl's. And sometimes two jars would explode with light at the same time. When we put the makeshift lanterns on the post, it was story time.

The fence itself was unremarkable: two ten-foot wooden beams that could snap like toothpicks at any given moment. Three posts, all angled in different directions and surrounded by high crabgrass, held up the wooden beams. The fence separated our lawn from the Shillings'. It was rickety to its core, and only one of us could sit on it at a time. Sometimes we'd sit rapturously; sometimes we'd be bugging—the art of taking a long stiff blade of grass and poking it into one of the thousands of small delicate holes in the wood. Usually the grass would find its way into an insect tunnel and poke out from another hole inches away. But on luckier times, we would hit the jackpot and displace a large black termite from its hiding place. Double jackpot was when we found one with wings.

The beauty of these evenings lay in their complete informality and scattershot agenda. We really never knew when a tackle football game could break out or one of us would complain loudly that he hadn't been able to stay up to watch Night Gallery the night before. But there was one thing that summer that never changed: We were all in that brief and wondrously shielded period called boyhood—skinny, heads full of wonder, and on a strict diet of Wacky Pack gum and Table Talk Pies. We talked of sex, Matchbox cars, and how just about anyone could escape from those flimsy bamboo jails in Planet of the Apes…but mostly we talked of sex. The fence post was a haven for low-toned conversations about how babies were born, and none of them ever began with the words when a mommy loves a daddy. The three of us were light-years ahead of such G-rated material. We had plunged into R without any parental guidance whatsoever.

Shilling was a chubby youth who we really didn't consider fat—I think the term most used was big-boned. If there was a strongman among us, he was it. Shilling was usually unkempt, with uncombed blond hair and a goofy, gap-toothed smile that made him look guilty no matter the circumstance. Shilling's shirts were sometimes tie-dyed, and we all marveled at the freaky designs and loud colors. He was cool and our chief storyteller—our ringmaster for the night's entertainment, unless Hurl or I had an update about any girls, which was never. When he sat atop that fence and looked at us with that you-gotta-hear-this grin, we gazed at Shilling like the apostles looked at Jesus in our Sunday school books.

On this glorious night, the frogs were loud, the air was still, and Shilling did not disappoint. He was in trouble—so much so that it was a marvel he'd been allowed out that evening. Shilling had a brother named Ty, a self-made delinquent two grades ahead of us who was already a school-yard legend for repeatedly missing classes and getting poor grades.

Unlike some derelict brothers, Ty wasn't mean, but he was always absent. He was barely around in the daylight hours, so after school, we would walk into his empty bedroom and gaze at all the Jimi Hendrix and The Who posters tacked to the wall. These small boxes called Zig-Zag were always on his desk, and his ashtrays were always filled with seeds, not ash. Occasionally we would pick one up and wonder what all the fuss about pot was about.

Like our rooms, however, there were similarities, including clothes scattered about the floor, sometimes two dirty underpants deep. There were Playboy magazines clumsily hidden under the bed, as if anyone who looked would not see the tattered covers immediately. And there were a few Aurora monster models, but his looked old and dusty and were hidden in the corner, as if he didn't play with them anymore. Hurl and I always coveted his masterpiece, the Creature from the Black Lagoon. There was only one word to describe Ty's detailed painting of the plastic beast: boss.

That night on the fence post, Shilling told the lawn-mower story. I can't remember the exact words, but I will never forget his faces, expressions, and gestures during his performance. One Saturday morning, Ty was busy doing nothing, but he had committed to a job as some kind of professional lawn mower. Ty, of course, was too lazy and gave the job to Shilling.

Ty said, "You'll make forty bucks. No one has seen me before, so just answer to my name, and you'll be OK. No prob. Have fun, bro."

"Why can't you do it, Ty?"

Ty had to think for a second—he was running thin on excuses. "I forgot I promised to take Katy to the beach...and that will pay off tonight. Know what I mean, bro?" He winked like an idiot.

"When does it start?" Shilling gave up on the argument that would have followed and took the job.

"Uh, right now," Ty uttered through a mouthful of Lucky Charms.

The job lasted less than one day, mainly because Shilling was ten and didn't know what he was doing. In fact, at the end of his abrupt shift, Shilling could have ended up in one of many places: the hospital, stranded deep in the woods, or even in jail.

It seemed Shilling's temporary supervisor was a burly Paul Bunyan of a figure named Gunnar. Everybody around town would see Gunnar cutting lawns with machines, although his muscular frame made it look like he could have done it with only an ax and an ox named Babe. He always nodded and spoke very little.

The job had come around because Ty had answered an ad in the local newspaper. Gunnar had called him up and asked a few questions, but there were only two big requests. Gunnar asked, "Do you know how to use a Locke mower?" and "Can you drive truck?"

Ty answered yes with authority. He was very practiced in the art of deception. When carded at the local package store for a six-pack of beer, he would say, "Of course I'm eighteen, and I'm late for my fishing trip" with the best of them.

According to Shilling, the day started out fine. Gunnar's truck pulled in front of the house and rumbled in the driveway for ten minutes. Shilling wolfed down his bowl of Cheerios and ran outside. Gunnar's powerful old Ford was shaking the ground. The passenger door was higher than that of any vehicle Shilling had ever climbed into. He opened the door, and Gunnar nodded as he ate an egg sandwich. Shilling noticed most of the egg had squished out and landed on the floor.

Gunnar gave Shilling a nod of respect. "You sure you're old enough for this son?"

Shilling had no idea whatsoever but lied, as Ty would have, "Yes, sir."

As they got going, it was already hot, and the old Ford wheezed from the heat. It didn't seem to bother Gunner though. He was wearing a ripped T-shirt that made Shilling a little uncomfortable. The first time you meet a man, you don't want to see his belly button.

"You sleep OK?" Gunnar asked. Barely.

"Fine. You?" replied Shilling, too nervous to really care.

"Need to stop at the Superette for some smokes before we head off into Wilton." Gunnar spit out the window. "Gotta do the lawn of some movie star. He's off in France or something. Pays a fortune as long as we do it perfect."

Shilling gulped. Wilton was the land of million-dollar houses that had pools, tennis courts, and even some paddle tennis courts. He would often see homeowners playing little games of tennis in the middle of winter as he drove home. It was weird, and looked like what the Beverly Hillbillies would be doing.

Finally they reached their destination. It was nothing special, really—kinda small, but the lawn was big. The house was also surrounded by beautiful rose bushes. Gunnar stopped the truck on the gravel driveway. They both got out and lowered the back gate. There it stood: the Locke mower, resembling something more capable of harvesting bales of wheat than cutting lawns.

"Grab that two-by-four," Gunnar said, referring to the long piece of wood on the interior of the truck. Both men, or shall we say man and boy, hoisted the wood with a grunt. Gunnar placed the boards directly under the Locke's wheels. He got up in the truck and slowly brought the beast down like an Arabian show horse. It was magnificent.

Gunnar said, "Well, here she is, Ty. And I'll teach you how to use this, knowing you lied to me—no kid knows how to use a Locke mower at your age."

Shilling panicked. "Well, I've seen them operated on the side of the road."

For the first and only time, Gunnar smiled, "It's OK, son. She's big. But she behaves, and I have the confidence you two will get along just fine."

Shilling smiled back. Also for the first and only time.

Gunnar climbed back up into the truck and picked up a regular-sized lawn mower, which he carried above his head.

"Above his head!" Shilling bragged to us at the fence post.

Gunnar put the little mower down gently. "This I know you've used before," he said.

Shilling said, "Yes, sir." It was true he could operate that baby in his sleep after mowing his yard at home so many times. Shilling went over and stroked the small mower as if it were a loyal pet. It was a Toro, a different model from his dad's but still very manageable.

Gunnar began the bonding session. "Gonna quickly train you on the Locke first. You can start in front there—it's smooth and level. The back is rocky, so I use this little Toro one to cover that."

Gunnar grabbed the handlebars of the Locke and started her up. She sounded like a small plane, and Shilling covered his ears. Gunnar put on a pair of big earmuffs. "Did you bring anything for your ears?"

Shilling shook his head.

Gunnar continued, "You can use these."

Back at the fence post, as this story was unraveling, Hurl, Jeremy, and I were already on the grass, laughing.

"Wait. Wait," said Shilling. "It gets better…or actually, it gets worse."

According to Shilling, here's how it went: The Locke mower moved smoothly, and he had no problems, even over the stony road. Shilling thought it was probably the Cadillac of lawn mowing machines. He imagined the long blades hidden underneath chopping like a million grass clippers. Shilling stood at its helm, much like a cabin boy at a giant ship's wheel.

"This handlebar has the brake," Gunnar said. "Just like the brake on your bike, yes?"

Shilling cocked his head as if he were a parakeet learning a first word.

"This other handlebar makes it go! Just like a motorcycle. Watch." Gunnar released the brake, and there she went, all smooth and powerful. Gunnar looked back at Shilling, "She's all bark and no bite. You try it."

Gunnar squeezed the brake and made room for Shilling. He got to the podium of the machine and carefully switched hands with Gunnar. Shilling stood there, looking over the front of the machine like a small elderly woman would gaze out the window of a large Buick. Gunnar gave Shilling the thumbs-up like he was on a tarmac. Shilling slowly let go the brake and felt the power of the beast propel him forward almost into a trot. It was too fast. Shilling quickly went into brake mode.

Gunnar came over and put a hand on Shilling's shoulder. "You'll get the hang of it! As you can see, the lawn is really square. Just keep going back forth, but whatever you do, don't go near the rose bushes. Give me at least five feet, so we can trim with the Toro. I'll be back before lunchtime."

Shilling felt both manly and pee-in-your-pants scared.

"Oh yeah…use these." Gunnar handed Shilling the earmuffs. And that was it. Gunnar was already around the corner. Shilling stared at the muffs, which were already sweaty and smelly and had pieces of dried food in them. He threw them on the grass and began cutting.

The Locke mower was having its way with Shilling—no different from a baby carriage pushing around a mom. He could stop and turn the mower, but when it was cranking full steam, he had a hard time keeping up. Once his shorts fell down, and he let go of the mower, only to find it was still hauling down the lawn. Quickly Shilling pulled his pants up past his now-green tube socks, which had been pristine white an hour earlier. He caught up to the mower and sighed in great relief. But questions began to arise: How do I turn this thing off? How do I get water? What if I gotta pee?

An hour later Gunnar came lumbering around the corner. He frowned at some of the crooked lanes but looked over the rest of the lawn and seemed pleased. Shilling was plenty relieved at this point to have some help.

Gunnar thrust his gloved hands just below Shilling's chest and flicked a switch. The machine stopped, but the metal gears kept spinning and slowly began to wind down until Shilling could hear life again. Birds chirping. Cars rushing late for the train station to New York.

Gunnar was gracious. "Good. Let's have an early lunch?"

It was only ten thirty, but Shilling didn't complain.

Gunnar asked, "You know how to drive a truck with a stick shift?"

Shilling knew he had to appear capable. "Yes, sir."

Gunnar eyed him suspiciously. He said, "There's a deli down the road. Get me a tuna sandwich, a quart of Bud, and a pack of Camel smokes, and I'll pay for your lunch today—being the first day on the job—or anything you want. Except a girl for the night. Ha ha." Gunnar shoved his elbow into Shilling's shoulder.

"Thanks, Gunnar," Shilling said.

Gunnar handed Shilling the keys to the truck. They had a *Hell no. I won't go!* metal ring attached to them. The Locke mower started up again. Gunnar turned to Shilling and asked, "Where are my earmuffs?"

Shilling pointed to the place where he'd dropped the decrepit things. The big man walked over, picked up the ear muffs, and put it on his head. Shilling watched him expertly cut around the prized rose bushes as a professional manicurist would. He thought someday he could learn to do that and walked to the side of the house where the truck was.

This is where the trouble began.

Shilling walked around the old truck like a proud papa. He kicked the wheels as he had seen his dad do a million times before. But this was an old and fairly large truck. And persnickety. Shilling walked over to the driver's side and opened the door. He stepped up on the running board and got behind the wheel. He sank into the seat like it was his dad's old recliner; it was like quicksand for his butt. He could see maybe five inches of daylight through the front windshield. The seat was down so low the gear shift reached up to his chest. Shilling started the lumbering thing. The engine revved. He was sure R meant reverse, so he moved the shift stick in that direction…except there were three pedals underneath his feet. Demon thing. In a breathtaking frenzy, something clicked, and the truck was suddenly going backward at thirty miles per hour. Shilling was flying blind. The mirrors were too tall for him to use. Branches were coming through the window and scratching whatever paint was left on the truck. He panicked and took a guess at which pedal was the brake.

RA-DUMP.

The loudest sound yet.

Shilling took his feel off the pedal, and the gears grinded to a hasty halt. He sat there and thanked all his dead uncles, grandmothers, God, and Jesus. He sat there a minute, wheezing like a ninety-year-old man. The Locke mower was still roaring up front.

"What was that ra-dump?" he asked himself. He got out, and the joyous birds started getting on his nerves. He circled the old thing. No dents. No holes. Shilling let a peep of relieved air out of his mouth. He kicked the tires again, this time in frustration. He put his fist down on the hood—he was never going back in that thing. Suddenly his pudgy frame froze like a stick figure you'd see scribbled in a school notebook. What would he do about lunch? What about the pack of Camels? And the big Bud…

That's when he saw it.

Shilling rolled under the truck and saw the Toro mower smashed beyond all recognition. It was flattened like a Frisbee—a crime that would go severely punished.

Think, think, Shilling thought. The Locke was still mulching out front. Shilling got on his belly, acting quickly. There was very little time. He pulled out the sad thing. Gasoline leaking onto his bony hands. He took the Toro and ran deep into the woods with it—at least a hundred yards—and flung it into a small creek. He covered the pathetic machine with leaves just to be sure, feeling as though he was hastily burying a dead body with the cops on his trail. He bent down to the creek and washed his hands. Shilling smoothed out his pants, wiped any dirt from his shirt, slicked back his hair, and realized the Locke mower's sound was gone. He ran back out and knew he had absolutely no plan. He began scheming for what would always be known now as the dumbest thing any kid had ever done.

Gunnar was wringing his hands. He wiped the sweat from his dripping, long blond mane. Shilling wondered if he should just tell the truth and take his medicine. He went around front and told Gunnar he couldn't drive the truck. Gunnar had seen the truck backed up poorly and guessed as much.

"OK, just mow the back with the small mower. I'll be done in twenty minutes," Gunnar grunted. Shilling dutifully walked back, praying he wouldn't drop a load in his pants. For the longest twenty minutes in his life, he paced and felt his stomach grumble something fierce. It was clear to him that he would spend the next ten years in Sing Sing. Gunnar came back with the Locke and looked around again with a sigh. "Why didn't you mow that back lawn?"

Shilling said absolutely unconvincingly, "I…I couldn't find the mower. Weird. I…I looked all around."

"What?" Gunnar asked.

"Yeah, it was just gone. Maybe someone stole it?"

Gunnar looked around at the peaceful, quiet lane and shook his head. Something was wrong in the state of Denmark. Gunnar was not a scholar, but he was not an idiot. "Help me with the gate and the ramp."

They walked around to the back and pulled up the truck door, then laid the planks back down. Gunnar started his mower and drove it up inside. Then he came down on a mission. He gazed around the truck and walked around the backyard. Shilling looked up at the sky like a fool. He even managed a pathetic guilty whistle. Gunnar walked to the front yard.

Whew, Shilling thought. The Toro wasn't even close by. He was free and clear.

Suddenly Gunnar went toward the back woods, getting closer.

Shilling was still hoping Gunnar would come to the conclusion that aliens had taken the mower to study Earth's engineering capabilities.

Gunnar took a right. He was still a ways away, but he clearly wasn't going to give up and say, "Well, the heck with it. Someone must have swiped it. Let's go home."

Gunnar was getting closer.

The woods were silent. Gunnar was out of view.

Closer.

Shilling just stood there, waiting for the inevitable.

Closer.

Then he heard Gunnar scream, "What the fuck? Owwwwwwwwwww. You idiot!" The giant man walked out with the Toro mower, cradling it like a dead dog. "Get in the truck," he said.

They drove home. Not a word. They pulled up to the driveway.

"You owe me one hundred bucks. I'll expect it by the end of the summer," Gunnar said.

Shilling got out of the truck, ran into his bedroom, and got under the bed. He heard the muffled tones down below of the brute man and his dad discussing the heinous crime.

As Shilling was just about done with his story of utter buffoonery, I heard my mom calling me home for the third time. I was up that night giggling until the wee hours, knowing full well to never take a lawn-cutting job with a man named Gunnar.

Tante

Summer always arrived with a honk in the Foxton boys' universe. That honk usually came at around eight in the morning the day after school let out for the summer. Tante would pull up and beep her car horn to let the whole neighborhood know she had arrived. My brother and I would jump out of bed, pajamas and all, ready to help Tante unload her stuffed piñata of an automobile. We'd run out the front door, printing fresh grass stains on our PJs. Mom would yell from her bed, "Put on your shoes," two minutes too late.

Tante's arrival signaled trips to the beach, fairs, hamburgers on the grill, and maybe just a present or two for my brother and me. We got to her car door before she could open it. Her smile was infectious, and we could do nothing but jump up and down like babies reaching for a mobile. (If anyone had seen such behavior, schoolyard beatings would have been dealt out swiftly, but no one was looking, so we threw caution to the wind.) The door opened. "Boyz. Boyz. Chim. Cheremy."

Tante was of German descent, so *Cheremy* was *Jeremy*, and *Chim* was *Jim*. Her proper name was Katherine, but one time she'd told us of her distant Aunt Tante, and the name Tante had stuck. She wasn't a "Grandma," anyway.

Tante was as much of a hero to my brother and me as Batman or The Monkees. She was eighty-nine, and we knew that was old, but Tante would play Monopoly with us, jump in piles of leaves, and get into water-balloon fights. We knew time was not on our side with her, especially with Mom telling us, "You know, Tante is not a little girl anymore."

"She's not a girl, Mom—she's one of us," we would usually reply.

Mom would shake her head at our response and at the woman who had the energy of a twelve-year-old.

This year, though, Jeremy and I took a little punch to the stomach as we saw Tante looking, for the very first time, visibly frail. I could almost hear her bones creak as she gingerly slid out of her car and hugged us. My arms reached all the way around her, and I knew there was no way I could have done that the year before—she ate too many of her secret-batch chocolate chip cookies. It also seemed the black makeup around her eyes was more to hide something than to make her look pretty.

I dwelled on that thought for a half second until I could smell the cookies and kuchen. We saw the tins in the back seat, along with her luggage and some machine we'd never seen before. It had tubes and wires and seemed like some old-person device made for other grandmothers, not for Tante. We figured it must be for a friend or a secondhand store—Tante was a secondhand-store junkie. Tante would buy us pants, and I'd say to Mom, "How do we know someone didn't do a number two in these pants?"

"We'll wash them real good when we get home," she'd say as I made an *ewwwww* face.

In the back of Tante's car, we saw boxes wrapped with Fourth of July paper. We could always count on one or two packs of bottle rockets, much to Mom's dismay. But by the time it was dark on the Fourth, Dad and Mom usually had a few cocktails and didn't care if we fired off nuclear bombs, as long as we pointed them at the Shillings' house across the street. Dad and Mr. Shilling had a lawn-off every summer, and sometimes the competition got downright funny. The whole family, including Mom, would look out the window and laugh at them mowing lawns on Saturday mornings as they wore headbands, wristbands, knee braces, and ridiculously colored pants hoisted so high you could have switched them with Mom's panties and no one would have known the difference.

Tante walked slowly toward the house, and at that moment, for the first time, she looked like a senior citizen.

I know very little about her life, but what I do know is that she came over from Germany to work in 1929. And work she did: ten hours a day at a bakery. Sometimes she would babysit for neighboring families after that, and she was only nineteen at the time. That's when she met my grandfather, Emil. I never knew him—he died when I was three—but I heard he was the same way. Emil was a machinist of some kind and came home around eight every night, barely able to mutter a sentence. Some nights it was so bad Tante had to undress Grandpa and put him in the shower. Afterward he would kiss her good night. Right after that he would open his window shade, point his fist in the direction of his shop, and slowly raise his middle finger. Then he'd put his head on the pillow and begin snoring until the alarm rang at five o'clock.

When Tante visited us, it was all business at first. She would trim the bushes, take the lawn mower down to the creek, and whack at the weeds. Mom would make lemonade for me to take down to Tante. Usually she would stop the lawn mower, look at the tray, and say to me, "You have it, Chim; I'm coming in for lunch soon."

I'd run back to the house to report this to my family, who looked on in both wonder and bemusement at her superhero efforts. She was eighty-nine years old that summer. I added it up, and she had lived more years than the entire family combined. No wheezing. No complaining. She was a machine.

That grand day Tante finally finished her chores and made her entrance into the kitchen by the back screen door with a loud "whooo." We all erupted with cheers and laughter and, truth be told, a little guilt.

On those nights my dad always made the same thing: a big steak on this little grill everyone was buying called a hibachi. Looked like a stupid thing to me. How're you supposed to cook six cheeseburgers on this little thing all at once? We sat down for dinner, and Tante frowned at the meat. She didn't approve, I guess. Maybe she didn't have it like that as a kid. Or even at home. I don't think she had as much money as my dad. Tante just filled her bowl with the usual salad, picked at some vegetables, and had a large iced tea. We always made fun of her superstrength, and she said it was her German genes.

"You better hope you have those genes, Chim and Cheremy." She would wave her finger.

Yeah, yeah, yeah, we thought...until we were about fifty.

Tante would go take what she called a quick nap. She slept for twenty minutes. On the dot. After that it was present time.

We'd gather in the living room and open the usuals. My brother and I would find our explosives and hide them from Mom as quickly as possible in fear of confiscation. My dad would smile at the knitted sweater. And this was a genuine smile—Tante was a serious sweater maker.

Mom got a knitted blanket for the bed and gave me a look. The year before I'd been playing on Mom's bed and chewing Dubble Bubble—like twice the legal limit of Dubble Bubble. As I jumped, it fell out, and a Cat in the Hat scenario broke out as my feeble attempts to pull the pink goo off just kept getting messier and messier. Soon there was more Dubble Bubble than wool. Mom's stern look was justified.

Tante then pulled out a small envelope from her pocketbook. "Chim, I forgot your birthday in January. Tante is getting a little old with these things," she said, smiling sweetly. She handed me the envelope. The cover said *TO: Master James Foxton.*

I had never been called *Master* before. That caught my eye, as did the return address of Warren Publishing in Santa Rosa, California. I had seen this address before. My heart began to surge. Tante looked at me like I was a baby again. Her eyes were full of tears. I tore open the card and read the inscription:

Master James Foxton
You are subscribed for a year
Famous Monsters Magazine.

Now *this* was something. Every Saturday night for as long as I could remember, I had watched Creature Features or Chiller Theater, depending on the film being shown. In the summer no one bothered me about staying up late. Jeremy would join me, and we would be transfixed on *The Crawling Eye* as Forest Tucker battled giant space mutants with tentacles and large eyes in the cold Alps.

Of course there were the classic Universal monsters, but over the years, I had seen them so many times that, at this point in my life, I was bridging out to stranger fare. The one that really got me, the one that put the lights on in my room for half a year, was Charles Laughton in *The Island of Lost Souls*. Quite frankly, I thought Channel Five had made a mistake in showing this movie so early at night as I watched in true, openmouthed, sweaty horror.

And now I was discovering these guys from England, such as Christopher Lee and Peter Cushing. Some kids are born athletes. Some are gifted with numbers. My fields of excellence were horror, Halloween, practical jokes like fake dog poop, fake barf, and soon my mom's Kodak Super 8 camera to make movies with.

However, Tante's gift of *Famous Monsters* was something special. This meant she had finally given in to my love of Boris Karloff over Charles Dickens or Beethoven. Usually, at least three times during a showing of Creature Features, she would come into the den and huff and puff about how we should be reading, complaining about how we were wasting the brains the Good Lord had given us.

"How your mother and father let you watch this is beyond me," she'd say. Her thick German accent made it especially funny, but my brother and I would save our laughs until she left the room.

This gift was nothing less than a treaty of peace, which made it even more special. I didn't cry, but my eyes were moist. I leaped up off the floor and hugged her somewhat skeletal body.

"I am giving this to you because you somehow have some unnatural ghoulish attraction to this stuff, Chim," she said. "I know that *Frankenstein* and *Dracula* are great books, and I hope you read them someday. I love you, *butzlemouse*." (*Butzlemouse* was a German name of affection that no one else said but her.)

I hugged her again, and it never occurred to me that this woman who was such a pillar in our lives would become sicker with each week of the summer.

By August things would never be the same.

The Adman and the Omega Man

EVERY YEAR ON JULY 3, Dad would take me into New York City, where he worked. I didn't have a lot of Dad time during the year, and I looked forward to this jaunt into the big-building, hot dog vendor and pizza-joint jungle with great anticipation. Mom always told us our dad was some kind of creative genius. We had no idea what that meant except he provided us with a pretty comfy life. We knew nothing more about his profession except he did those Volkswagen commercials on TV. He worked in TV, which was great because TV was my life.

Occasionally I would see one of his commercials and get mildly excited until *Voyage to the Bottom of the Sea* came on, and then I would get very excited. Every Sunday night we would all gather 'round the TV, transfixed for an hour of glorious undersea adventure and monsters made out of household carpet. On Wednesday nights *Batman* was my favorite until it got canceled. I loved the Joker, Riddler, and King Tut, and my favorite, of course, was Egghead because he was played by Vincent Price. This was forty years before comic-book villains actually became cool. Comic-Con was a long way off.

To get to New York, my dad and I would wait at the Saugatuck train station for the 8:20 a.m. New Haven to Grand Central Terminal line. It was ninety degrees, and he was still wearing a hat. Mom said it was too hot to wear a hat, but I think it was because my dad was losing his hair and was not quite ready for the comb-over.

During the colder days, he would wear a black suit, a red tie, and his trademark long Burberry raincoat, and even I could tell he was a badass businessman back then.

Standing there on the platform, I loved to look down that train line leading to who knew where. Was Chicago that way? Or Los Angeles *that* way? A few scattered souls with grumpy morning faces waited alongside us. I guessed most everyone had the day off because the next day was the Fourth of July.

Occasionally I would ride in the car with my mom to drop my dad off at the station, and there were so many commuters there was no room to stand. I often wondered how many people they could they stuff onto these trains.

But not today. This was a put-your-leg-up-on-the-seat-across-from-you kind of ride. "The best there is," Dad would tell me. He would usually go over the highlights for the day before we even started moving. I think he was as excited to show me his workplace as I was to visit.

It would always begin like this: "OK, Jim, we'll get to the big train station, then go to my office, and then have lunch. Whatever food you like. They have every kind of food in the world in New York. Any thoughts?"

It was always a no-brainer. "Indian," I'd say.

Two years earlier I'd been dragged to an Indian restaurant kicking and moaning, thinking I was going to eat spider eggs off the floor. Then I'd had my first taste of butter chicken curry. I can only say my mouth experienced a sensation akin to what those cowboys must have tasted when they smoked a Marlboro cigarette on TV: pure flavor country. My sophomoric palette had woken up.

My dad smiled. I think he might have been in the mood for a little Indian food as well. He then continued with the itinerary. "We'll walk down Fifth Avenue, past the giant lions at the library, then go to Times Square and see the lights, but you have to hold my hand there, Jim. I know you're a big boy, but there's muggers and thieves waiting to take our money." Which was true.

"Can we go see *The Omega Man*?"

My dad was no movie slouch either. "Charlton Heston vs. vampires. Count me in."

At the train station's magazine shop, they didn't have *Famous Monsters* magazine, but they did have the inferior *Castle of Frankenstein*. I'd had five dollars to spend, and now sixty-five cents of that were gone. What a scam.

The New Haven train rounded the corner with what seemed like an unnecessary whistle blow, since hardly anyone was there. It stopped with a fingers-on-the-chalkboard squeak.

We took our seats immediately, and I never once opened my *Castle of Frankenstein* on the whole trip. The ride was one of the best parts of the day—I could look outside and see the world beyond my little bubble of a street passing by. We stopped at little towns called Darien and Greenwich. There was even a city called Stamford. But the most interesting parts to me were the run-down places, such as Norwalk and parts of New York. This held nothing less than pure fascination and a bit of terror for me. Most of the buildings were brick. There seemed to be a lot of giant ads on the buildings that were either half torn down or so dirty you couldn't even read them anymore. And it always seemed to look hotter in these places. I don't know if that was because the people walking around seemed to wear less clothes: muscle shirts. Miniskirts. Basketball shorts. Kids ran through water spouts on city streets. Things seemed to move faster. It was exciting to see a whole other world.

The train eventually went through a very long, dark tunnel. I could hear and feel the roar of other trains in the distance. The poles rushing by were corroded and dank, and I spotted a ton of chip bags, newspapers, and cigarette packs strewn about the floor.

The train pulled up to the platform with an abrupt halt. A man in a blue suit and hat came through our door, announcing, "Grand Central Terminal, Grand Central."

Dad took me by the hand, saying he didn't want me to get lost.

"Are there muggers and thieves here too?"

"Jim, this is New York—they are everywhere. Have to be careful."

It seemed like a million people got off at Grand Central Terminal. They all got pushed together, and I couldn't see anything except the backs of heads. Hundreds of them. Short hair. Long hair. Huge hairdos. And hats everywhere. We finally made it past the throng and found ourselves in the most wondrous room I had ever seen, a cavernous place with a big clock smack-dab in the middle. The room was filled with the sounds of people murmuring, the announcements of other trains on the loudspeaker, men selling peanuts and newspapers, and a great ceiling. Oh my gosh.

I had to go to the bathroom, but my Dad wouldn't let me go. "There are bad people in the bathrooms here." I didn't understand why he was so cautious about many places in New York back then, but now I do. It was a beautiful place. It was also a rough place.

We got to the revolving door and went around. On the other side, the world opened up to me. The first thing I noticed was the smell. The staleness of hot steam came from below us. There was also the aroma of hot dogs, and I smelled other people smells, such as perfume. I smelled flowers and garbage too.

I always looked above first and marveled at the tall skyscrapers. Nothing in TV or movies ever prepared me for this. It almost made my knees weak. My dad still had me by the hand, and I was glad. The cars, mostly yellow, were screeching, and people yelled at the cars in front of them, who yelled at the cars in front of them. Every store had something cool in the window. Even the ladies' clothes stores were neat, because there were scenes of people in the winter or playing on the beach.

We passed so many guys with carts selling nuts I would lose count. The one thing I never enjoyed about the city is that it was steamy. Hot, yes, but this was more of a sweaty humidity, like I was in some prehistoric landscape. I would look up often and see Dad wipe the back of his neck with a handkerchief.

Compared to all the other grand structures, my dad's building was unspectacular. It felt gray and kinda dirty until you went inside. And when you passed through the regular doors (disappointingly not revolving doors), the world was once quiet again.

On the right side of the lobby was a store. Imagine that: Right in your building was a place you could buy candy and Cokes and stuff. This was the kind of thing I could boast about to my friends. We also passed a barbershop with a swirling red-and-white pole. It had two comfy-looking seats outside the shop, and I guessed they were for shoe shining. Whenever we passed by, it always smelled like the stuff Mom used to clean the kitchen floor.

My dad would press the elevator button, the door would open, and we'd be whisked up to some floor higher than fifty. My stomach would always flutter on this part of the trip.

But when the doors opened, it was a wonderland.

No longer was the inside of the building gray; it was white. The walls were white. The receptionist's desk was white. The lamps. The chairs. Only the carpet was a bright red.

And let me tell you why: Dad worked at the greatest ad agency in the world at this time. The name was Fritz, Lunger, and Bailey. They did all the good commercials you would see on TV, the ones that made you laugh. My dad said this place was a mecca for creativity for the most talented ad people in the world. Everybody in advertising wanted to work here. Everybody.

"Your dad is very lucky," he said.

As we walked down the pristine halls, I could hear people laughing. I saw a paper airplane fly out of a doorway. My dad would say hello, and they would reply, "Hey, Connecticut Hal." I guess at Fitz, Lunger, and Bailey there were no days off, because people were everywhere.

Dad led me to his office, and it was something indeed. There was a desk, and there were chairs, and there was even a couch. But there were drawings all over the wall with words on them like, "How does the plower get to his snow plow?" Below there was a crude sketch of a car. *Yeah*, I thought, *how* does *a plower get to his snow plow?* Even at my age, I knew this was clever.

In the corner of the room lay a stack of Hot Wheels tracks. Eureka. The only drawback was that the cars he had were kinda bogus: Volkswagen buses and Beetles. No hot rods. His partner, Bill, would come in with a pad and a handful of Magic Markers. He'd put them on the floor and say, "Go at it, kid."

Then my dad and Bill would leave for what seemed like hours.

This day, however, was special. I was in for a rare treat.

An old man walked into Dad's office and smiled at me. He put out his hand and said, "Hi. I'm Mr. Bailey."

I heard my Dad talking about this man all the time. "Hi," I said back.

"Are you Hal's boy?"

I nodded.

"You're doing Volkswagen ads, I hope."

I chuckled nervously and said I wasn't. Then he got down on the floor next to me and sat cross-legged in his pinstripe suit. "Can I show you around here? See what we do?"

I nodded again, this time up and down like a monkey.

"First a couple runs down the Hot Wheels track, eh?"

I got up and grabbed those orange strips quickly. We both looked for a launching point and decided on my dad's desk. Mr. Bailey took the red tabs and connected the orange track. It was four strips—quite long, in my humble opinion.

He took the van. I took the Beetle. We placed them on top, overlooking the treacherous fall below. Mr. Bailey said, "Ready, set, go." The Beetle glided down the slippery slope and creamed the van. We did it again with the same result. I could tell Mr. Bailey was not pleased.

"I have to make some adjustments," he said.

I polished my car with my shirt, giving it a nice sheen. Mr. Bailey took a roll of masking tape off the desk. He also took a paperclip and affixed it to the top of the bus.

I was well versed in Hot Wheels unsanctioned makeovers, but this was Dad's boss. Who was I to argue?

We put the cars on the top, and the van went down the hill like a cheetah out of hell. It even skidded off the tracks and sailed into my dad's wall, making a little brown mark.

Mr. Bailey laughed. "I don't like to lose. But your car was better. You beat me fair and square." He rubbed the hair on my head. "C'mon, let me show you this place."

I walked around with wide-eyed wonder. Everywhere we went he was treated with the utmost respect. We entered a gigantic room where all they did was make posters. I saw rows and rows of desks with people typing. There was even a pool table. But the best part was a little movie theater they called a screening room. The seats were bright red and cushioned, not the kind of butt-breakers you would find at our local theater. There were only four rows, and the screen was right in your face no matter where you sat. There was a smell of old smoke in the air.

Mr. Bailey and I sat down, and he yelled, "Roll it."

On the screen came a silly commercial about a gorilla throwing around a suitcase, then another commercial that made me laugh, then another. It was amazing. This was a job? I wanted in. Even at age ten.

"This is what we do," he said. "You think you might like to come here and work someday?"

I didn't need to think. "Yes, sir," I answered.

He escorted me back to my dad's office, where Dad and Bill were arguing about something. Dad stopped midsentence and said, "Hello, Mr. Bailey."

"Good morning, Hal. Your son beat the crud out of me in Hot Wheels, and then I took him around. Hope you don't mind."

"No, sir." Dad looked slightly perplexed. I took it Mr. Bailey had more important things to do.

For lunch we had Indian food. I tried many things, and some were gross, but the vindaloo, samosas, and naan would keep me full for a week. Afterward the waiter gave me a hot mint. I was confused by this. The food was a little spicy, and I was being handed what was essentially a fireball? No Lifesavers? My dad unwrapped the hot candy and started sucking on it. I wanted to throw up, but somebody had already done it next to where we were walking.

We saw the great lions at the library. He shot film of me sitting on one of their backs. We stopped for a Coke and the best pretzel I'd ever had. It was warm and chewy and the size of my head. We also put mustard on it. In New York I always learned something new—and to this day, that hasn't changed.

We finally got to Times Square, my Beulah Land. There were camera stores next to more camera stores next to the best pizza I'd ever had. Next to that were movie theaters that had pictures of naked women. (This was outright bragging material for the fence post the next night.) Giant signs cried, *XXX. Nude Girls!* And funny titles of dirty movies, such as *Booby and Clyde, 2001 A Sex Odyssey*, and (my favorite) *Tits a Wonderful Life*. Guys who looked like they were part of the Joker's gang stood outside the theater smoking cigarettes, swapping money and stuff. A little farther up the street were the golden temples: huge movie theaters with titles Mom wouldn't even let me speak: things like *I Eat Your Skin* and *I Drink Your Blood* and finally *The Omega Man*.

The lights on the marquee were all blinking. There was no line. There never was for these movies, as there was at our miniature theaters in Westport, which always showed stuff like *Love Story* and *Fiddler on The Roof*. Occasionally a James Bond movie would come through and, of course, *Where Eagles Dare*. But these places were palaces. Before you even went in, the ceilings were fifty feet tall. And once you opened the door, the smell of popcorn and licorice almost knocked you over.

We bailed on the concession stand, both of us bloated from pretzels and palak paneer. Five doors spread about twenty-five feet apart each led to the theater. The lobby was carpeted, and you could tell it was getting run-down. Dreams in my head conjured up what this place used to be—a grand kingdom. Dad opened the door and ushered me in. All of a sudden, he grabbed the back of my shirt. On the movie screen, as big as a drive-in's, I saw a guy being ripped to shreds by ghouls.

"Whoa. Whoa. Whoa," Dad said. He hoisted me back into the lobby. "The first movie isn't finished yet. And don't tell your mom you saw that," he said sternly. He didn't have to. That was a moment I would keep locked up inside forever. How cool was that? My first real zombie movie!

We waited and went in for *The Omega Man*. I often asked myself how Charlton Heston went from being Moses or some big Bible guy to fighting monsters. Older people and I could carry on conversations about how great he was, and we'd be talking about different movies. The smile on my face during that one hour and thirty-eight minutes was as wide as the Grand Canyon.

Years later they cleaned up Times Square, and it is not the same as it used to be. It's bittersweet because I miss it, and I am sure glad my kids never saw all those sex shows and what I now know are called prostitutes. But I am also sure glad I got to see it. It was still light out when we went home and got back on the train. I missed all the cities and towns because I fell asleep on my dad's shoulder. Summer began on a high note.

She (Part 1)

THERE WERE TWO *SHEs* IN my life that summer, and both changed the view of my miniscule world. The first She was a Schwinn Stingray bicycle, and the second was Melissa Praddleton. I have to tell you about the bike first, for if not for that aluminum beauty, I would never have met Melissa and had my first interactions with obsession, desire, and humiliation.

I received the Schwinn in March for my birthday, that summer was when I really discovered the joy of being reckless and irresponsible on two wheels. I had all the accoutrement: the sissy bar, the banana seat, and the king of spades playing card pinned to my spokes for that rat-a-tat sound. The bike was gold and had hardly a scratch on her—that is, until it got warmer and the trails in the rocky woods became more passable. This is where we could build jumps that would test our imaginary shock absorbers as well as our courage. In other words, we could have died many times.

The summer of 1972 seemed especially green. The crickets sounded louder. The sun seemed hotter. It was going to be that one summer I'd always remember when I got older. As I rode down West Ambler Road with Hurl, Shilling, and Jeremy, we were nothing less than royalty. It was the pinnacle of youth, boyhood, and innocence. Older people on the street were afraid of us, and Mrs. Munson would "Hmmpprrh" at our reckless speed. The little kids would sit there with big round eyes, watching us like we were Greek gods who had just come from Mount Olympus for a jaunt.

The big question for all of us, however, was how far we could go. Biking from the comfort zone of your street onto the unfamiliar streets of the town was a scary proposal. There was a dividing line at the end of the asphalt on West Ambler Road, leading to a concrete two-lane street known as Turkey Hill. This barrier was not so much visible as it was emotional.

We knew, of course, what lay beyond, watching from the back seat of our parents' cars. But that was in the safety of a car—not alone on a bike with fast automobiles whizzing by; roving gangs of other bikers who loved to beat up kids like us; and haunted houses, monsters, and more. The cars also drove much faster on Turkey Hill than on West Ambler Road, and there was only a narrow dirt path on the right side of the road for bike travel. The big kids in the grades above ours were always riding their bikes out here on the road itself. But were we ready?

The four of us gathered at the bottom of West Ambler Road on the Fourth of July. We stood there on our rides at the end of the street like we were about to jump off the edge of the Grand Canyon. We looked out onto the side road ahead as if it were a ten-lane highway. Our parents would never have approved of such a trip, so we didn't bother to even ask them. It wasn't dishonest; it was just the way God made kids.

Our final destination? A rickety old general store called Borchette's. Borchette's was about a mile and a half down Turkey Hill and then a dreaded half mile on the Post Road. This was not a highway, but it was four lanes—a serious piece of roadway in a kid's eyes. A mess up or a wipeout on that street, and you might as well have been eaten by the giant ants in the movie *Them!* None of us would say it, of course, but this was man-up time.

Hurl ventured out first. His wheels were a little wobbly for the first ten yards, but then he gathered some speed and was off. Shilling followed, and I followed him, trailed by Jeremy. This was such strange terrain. On West Ambler I knew every pothole, dirt patch, and rock on the street. This narrow path was intimidating.

We were about twenty yards down Turkey Hill when a blue Corvette whizzed by at what seemed like the speed of sound. The wind from the car made us all grab the handles of our bikes especially tight. Then followed a station wagon with even more force, but we managed to stay on our bikes at a respectable speed. Shilling was the first to have the confidence to turn his head and look back at Jeremy and me, wearing a smile bigger than the one he'd had when we all first tried a Ho Ho. I gave it right back to him. I turned and saw Jeremy lagging a little, so I slowed down. The last half of the road was a tiny hill that appeared to us like a highway going up into the French Alps. We all began to climb the peak of Turkey Hill, standing up and pedaling. It was maybe a tenth of a mile long and a mild forty-degree incline, but I was huffing and sweating and could feel my legs beginning to burn. Up ahead Hurl and Shilling were slowing down. Hurl was winded, his rock-steady bike now shaking. I looked behind me and saw Jeremy—the smart one—had just bailed on the whole thing. He was walking his bike comfortably and safely behind us at about the same speed we were pedaling.

At the peak of Turkey Hill, we managed to take in our bravery and put fatigue behind us for a moment. We had done it. A new frontier was opened. We high-fived one another…until a full rush of cars flew by us on the Post Road. There was no way we would have the cojones to cross to the other side of this mammoth roadway. Luckily, Borchette's was on our side and had a sidewalk leading directly up to the dilapidated front door.

This part of the trip was a breeze. Jeremy even made it the whole way, giggling and keeping up with the group. We all had allowance change in our pockets and were ready to do some business with old man Borchette.

Borchette's was a throwback to the last century of consumerism. It was a one-man general store right out of *Bonanza*. His establishment was in an old white house that had been converted into a duplex of sorts. The right side was where he lived, and the store was on the left. Every other building on the Post Road was a larger establishment, car dealership, or restaurant. Old man Borchette was the last of the holdouts of the preindustrial age. His 1940s-style house was an oddity, but it held something more precious than gold: penny candy.

We pulled up to Borchette's and threw our bikes on the ground. At that age, this was not disrespectful to our property. It just made us look cooler. There were no bike stands or lock-up racks. Very rarely was a bike stolen. So we just hopped off. It's one of those things, like littering, I just look back on and shake my head about.

We stepped onto the creaky white porch, which was covered in paint chips the size of small dogs. The entrance was an old screen door. Even in the blazing heat, the door was never shut. A small fan on the counter toward the back of the store was all he needed.

We opened the ancient door. More creaks. Once we were inside, it was an oasis. On the far left side was a sunken Coca-Cola refrigerator stocked with Coke; Tahitian Treat; Squirt; Fanta; 7-Up; and—our favorite—Yoo-Hoo, a chocolate drink that masqueraded as a milkshake. It was an amazing con. Chocolate water. We were suckers.

Gathering around the freezer, we carefully made our picks. Behind the counter Borchette watched us with great interest. In the past we had ripped off a candy bar or two, and he knew it.

He was just too slow to catch us. Borchette must have been in his late sixties or even seventies and appeared to be a decrepit older and fatter version of Colonel Sanders. His wife used to be out in the store, but she had disappeared a year or two earlier. No one knew whether she was sick or dead. "Or chopped up in the freezer, displayed as roast beef," Hurl once declared.

Borchette wore a white shirt and a smock in case anyone wanted some cold cuts. His meats were world-famous—not for the quality but for the amount of flies that gathered around them in the display case. Even at our age, no one could fathom asking for a pound of ham that had been a Thanksgiving meal for a dozen insects. On top of the meat case were two huge glass bottles. These barrels were large enough to house a two-headed cow at a freak show. Both were difficult to see into due to the discolored water, but one was filled with eggs and the other with pickles the size of a baby's arm.

"What do you boys want?" Borchette would say in a way that reminded us of a bartender talking to an outlaw gang in the old west.

We'd reply, "Ah, nothin'."

"Well, make your selections and get out," he'd reply.

We were used to the discourtesy—mainly from Mrs. Munson, but almost anyone we encountered over a certain age thought we were hoodlums. We could have been in our Sunday best and still would have been looked at as a pack of feral kids running amok.

After the difficult and lengthy soda-selection process, we went right over to the candy section, avoiding the deadly meat counter unless one of us was on a dare. Once we wagered and coaxed Shilling into asking for a slice of ham and eating it right there. We watched in horror, as one would have watched a circus act in the 1930s, as the slithery piece of meat went down his gullet. Then he gagged like he'd just eaten a ladle full of mayonnaise. We all laughed until he collected the dimes he'd won from us on the bet.

Back then a large candy, like a bag of M&M'S or a Hershey chocolate bar, was five cents. Things like Table Talk Pies and Twinkies cost a little more. But our eyes were always glued on the penny-candy jars. This, we felt, was where our best value was, and sixty cents goes a long way with prices like that. Borchette would break out the small brown paper bags, and we would line up, asking for Atomic Fireballs, Jawbreakers, Tootsie Rolls, and rolls of SweeTARTS. The whole process took probably thirty minutes—exactly one half hour Mr. Borchette probably wished he had never had. We paid him, and we went on our way. Lord knows what Mr. Borchette did when that screen door slammed and the four hoodlums left his establishment. Spit in a cup? Curse? Hack up more of Mrs. Borchette? But we got what we wanted, and that's all that counted. There was only one problem: making it back home to the safety and warm embrace of West Amber Road.

We did. And after that we all started venturing beyond our street.

That afternoon we were doing doughnuts and wheelies in the parking lot of Saint Luke's, a Catholic church situated about a half mile from West Ambler Road. This was a destination approved by our parents. It was close. It was safe. And though my parents were Protestants, they felt being near a godly place couldn't hurt me or my brother.

Shilling was easily the finest bikesmith in the neighborhood. He could spin his bike around 360 degrees if he built up enough speed and slammed on the brakes in the dirt. Hurl was the master of the jump. We'd find a piece of plywood, make a ramp at a ridiculous angle, and try to get as much air as we could. On a bike Hurl was fearless. There was an *I don't care* aspect to him that I had known about since the Where Eagles Dare night, but the others had no idea and put his bravery right up there next to Evel Knievel's.

After a while our little show began attracting a small crowd of kids who wanted to see our stunts and, more importantly, see one of us wipe out. Jeremy had a cloth and a can of WD-40 and would wipe down our bikes before each stunt. It was pure theatrics. After a few stunts, we would go over to appease the throng. That was where I saw Bobby Praddleton, but more importantly, this was the first time I laid eyes on Melissa—the other She.

Bobby was in our grade, and we feared him. He was one of the best athletes and was always picked second in kickball and four square after Hurl. Bobby had perfect blond hair and blue eyes and was the son of a prominent doctor in town. His house had a pool and sat on one of the nicest streets in Westport. My mom would always drive by there, looking at the homes and probably dreaming of having a tennis court, hosting parties, and hiring a maid.

"What are you losers doing?" Bobby sneered.

"Nothing you could do," I said and immediately got a high five from Shilling.

Bobby smiled and said, "Watch this, retards," as he rode his bike toward the ramp area. Bobby had brought his own cheering section—a few goons who lived off his popularity like leeches—and someone else. She was tall. Tan. Had a different look to her. Possibly from some other country? A stunning beauty. I wasn't the only one who had noticed. Hurl touched my arm and nodded toward the foreign wonder.

Bobby lined up for his ramp jump.

I was still looking at Melissa like she was a giant candied apple.

Bobby put his bike against a tree and stepped off. Then he proceeded to do a few body stretches as we rolled our eyes.

"Watch this, suckers!" Bobby commanded.

"Go, Bobby!" the princess yelled.

My heart sank. It was his girlfriend.

Bobby climbed back onto his bike, which was pristine in every way and twice as expensive as the Stingrays we rode. He began to pedal, and I could see the change in his eyes. They went from blue to black. His all-American smile became a grimace. This was a kid who did not like to look bad. He took the jump, and it was as graceful and high as any jump we'd ever done. He landed with the softness of an ice skater acing a triple axel. He looked at the crowd and tussled his blond curls. Everyone ran to congratulate him—even us. The stunt was that impressive.

"That was a nice jump, Bobby," I confessed.

"Thanks, Foxton." Bobby grinned in a way that was in no way friendly. And then he said four words I would dwell on for days: "You know my sister?"

I looked at the girl and somehow managed to smile even though she was a girl. I had never smiled at a girl before. Girls were just this other thing that sat next to the boys in school. We never played with them or collected baseball cards from them. The only time I ever learned about girls was watching TV. I knew they liked to laugh and play with an Easy-Bake Oven. That was it.

"Hi, I'm Jimmy." I held out my hand. This was a golden moment. Something huge was going to happen that would change my life.

Melissa smiled and said, "Hi. Bobby, can we go now?"

Ouch.

I introduced Hurl, Shilling, and my brother. I think we were all a little smitten. Melissa rode a pretty rad bike herself. It wasn't pink and didn't have tassels like other girls'; instead, it was bright red with a silver streak down the center.

"Melissa is in seventh grade. You've probably never seen her before." He was clearly showing her off. No way were they brother and sister. His white skin and her olive tone just didn't indicate they came from the same mother and father.

It was a Saturday night and getting late. I knew exactly when to be home for dinner, because my entire week revolved around what was on TV that evening.

"I gotta get back for dinner and Creature Features," I blurted out, hoping she would find me brave for watching things so scary.

"What's on?" Bobby asked.

"*Son of Dracula*. We've seen it a million times. Sucks," said Melissa of all people.

My mouth dropped open, not only because she said it but because she was right. *Son of Dracula* was a boring Lon Chaney Jr. vehicle to get him out of being forever typecast in the far superior *Wolfman* movies.

Bobby assumed his ridiculous bravado again and whistled. His gang and his sister gathered around his bike, and off they went. In the distance we could hear him say, "Losers," and laughter.

"What a dickhead," said Hurl.

"What a tool," Shilling said at the exact same time.

I just watched Melissa pedal out of my life. *A girl like that just doesn't know about Lon Chaney Jr. movies*, I thought. *It just doesn't happen.*

"His sister wasn't bad though," said Hurl.

"Nice boobs. Probably has a hundred boyfriends in junior high," Shilling responded.

Jeremy peeped up, "She doesn't look like she comes around from here. Maybe California."

We all nodded. Jeremy didn't speak that much, but when he did, it was unusually filled with wisdom—like a kid who was ten years old, not seven.

"All I know is I'd like to kick Bobby's ass," Hurl said, probably because his status as the master jumper had just been taken away from him.

"Fence post after dinner?" Shilling asked.

"Creature Features," I reminded him.

"Such a puss," he said to me, smiling.

The sun was slowly going down, and we all had dinner waiting for us. It was time to go and forget about Bobby Praddleton.

I did not know it then, but in two days, I would be a world away from him.

The Great Disney World Heist

THERE HAD NEVER BEEN A calculated robbery in the history of Disney World until July 1972, when Shilling and I got away with $23.47 in one of the most devious, shocking, and outlandish crimes in the annals of cartoon-based amusement parks. "It all started with a mouse," Walt Disney famously said. But for us it really all started with an announcement at the dinner table with Shilling and his parents.

"We have a surprise for you," Mrs. Shilling said, smiling like a sitcom mom. This was unusual for Mrs. Shilling, as she did not convey much emotion. In fact, her entire head could sit pretty comfortably with all the presidents atop Mount Rushmore.

"Your mother and I have decided to take you and a friend on a special vacation," Mr. Shilling chimed in next. Ty was luckily in Panama City, Florida, on the beach. Shilling failed to be enthused. The family vacation usually entailed an unholy amount of lengthy drives to places that weren't worth walking to. Case in point: the Cleveland Botanical Gardens. Basketville, the birthplace of the modern picnic basket. Or worse: the sheer horror of the candlemaker and silversmith exhibits in historic Williamsburg, Virginia. Shilling knew anything "historic" meant boring and might even be educational. No right-thinking boy wants to be learning while he's on summer vacation.

Mr. Shilling had just come home from work and still wore his signature sweat-stained white, short-sleeved T-shirt. He was getting a little too old to be standing outside construction sites nine hours a day. His rotund belly lay on the tabletop like three pounds of chopped sirloin on a butcher's scale. "In two days we are going to…Disney World! My boss couldn't go. His wife's uncle passed away. So my boss sold me the vacation. At a very good price, I must say," Mr. Shilling said, proud of himself.

Mrs. Shilling added, "This is the place where you can actually hug Mickey Mouse."

Shilling rolled his eyes. He knew the real highlights: Disney World was the place where you could ride an indoor roller coaster in space, scream in a haunted mansion, and whip around the Wild West on something called Thunder Mountain. Tales of this mystical place floated through the hallways of our school, usually after Christmas break, when the rich kids came back from their fancy vacations. Shilling and I had always promised each other that someday we would go.

So on July 6, 1972, we boarded a plane at JFK and landed in Orlando after a very long three hours and twenty-two minutes. Mr. Shilling rented a wood-paneled station wagon, and we drove to the Polynesian Village, the latest mega-resort built on the Disney World property. For its time, the structure was a masterful concoction of brick, mortar, and prefabricated bamboo. For an already bug-eyed pair of manic kids, it was just an unexpected dollop of emotional Cool Whip. Mr. Shilling drove up to the entrance. Shilling and I clung to the car windows like suckerfish in a tank.

Out front there were women in hula skirts. A fancy-looking man in a white suit hung leis around guests' sunburned necks. Mr. Shilling was already looking rested and smiling, and he was still in the driver's seat.

Shilling and I opened the doors before the car came to a halt.

"Any misbehaving and I'm sure there's a wooden spoon Mr. Disney can lend me to whack you with," Mrs. Shilling said with utter conviction. She would not be embarrassed by us on this grandest of excursions. She carried the memories of the last trip when Shilling and Ty had thrown water balloons from their hotel lobby onto a wedding down below. She knew the threat of the wooden spoon was all that was required to keep order this time.

The car came to a full stop, and Shilling and I exited the Ford gingerly. I still remembered seeing welts on Shilling's legs the size of New Haven and didn't want the wooden spoon. We leaped to the back of the car and grabbed the luggage, only to find a young man had already taken out the bags and put them on a cart. "Want a ride? Get on," he said.

We looked at Mr. and Mrs. Shilling for approval. We got it. I hopped in front and grabbed the polished gold support rails of the cart. Shilling sat in the back on the suitcases. Away we went with Christmas-morning smiles plastered to our faces.

Along the route we passed strange plants that begged to be touched. Giant wooden overhead fans reminded Shilling of tropical supper clubs in those old movies his parents watched on TV. Even the floor resembled something like the palace of a Tahitian king. It was made of polished wood inlaid with intricate carvings of Polynesian ceremonial masks.

But just beyond the glorious entrance of the hotel was the wonder of wonders: a footbridge that was no ordinary bridge. The behemoth teak structure had an arch that extended twenty feet above a lagoon filled with two-foot koi and generously sprinkled with water lilies. What caught Shilling's eye, however, was the shimmering glow just below the surface. Shilling looked quickly over at me. By this time I was in a state of certifiable glee. Shilling squealed like a pig boy and pointed at the bounty looming at the bottom of the man-made pond. There lay pennies, dimes, nickels, and even some quarters. I started mumbling some numbers aloud, and before I got to ten dollars, my math was interrupted by a pretty young girl and her father. The dad gave his daughter a nickel.

She raised it above her head and threw it mightily. "I wish that Mickey would give me his autograph," she said.

"Shhh. You should never let anyone hear your wish, or it won't come true," her dad advised, and he handed her another nickel.

Go ahead and add more to the money pool, Shilling thought. We were both already in scheming mode.

Mr. Shilling brought Shilling back to Earth with a pat on the back and a smile. The valet continued to push the baggage, and we rode in style toward the ornate front desk in the lobby. The Shillings stood in line with the other guests and just took it all in. In that moment the famed Disney advertising slogan was true: it was the happiest place on Earth.

Mr. Shilling had splurged for two rooms. Shilling and I were quick to grab room 207, which had a clear view of Lake Buena Vista and the Magic Kingdom shimmering on the other side of the waters like some kid nirvana.

For the next several hours, we walked the hotel property and cased the wishing pool. The robbery had to be pulled off that night. Shilling's parents would be busy unpacking, and then they would head to the patio area for the usual drinks and cigarettes.

As usual in late-summer Florida, it was annoyingly balmy. Men strolled with their families through the open-air lobby, sweating enough to show up on a Doppler radar. All the women blew hair out of their faces in unison, like a choreographed swimming team. Kids ran circles around their parents, staring at the tiki gods, outrigger canoes, and posters featuring drinks that looked like ice cream sundaes with little umbrellas in them.

It was time to execute.

Earlier, when doing our recon, we'd seen a security guard turn on the underwater lights behind the front desk for the koi pond. Both of us knew in order for any of this to succeed we must steal the coins in the dark. Shilling entered the lobby and put on his best *I am lost; will you please help me, mister?* look.

A hefty woman in an ill-fitting Cinderella costume approached almost immediately. "Why, you must be the eighth little dwarf," she said unconvincingly.

"I can't find my mom. She was just here," he said looking like one of those big-eyed cat paintings.

The Disney staff was a crackerjack unit when it came to connecting little boys and girls with their parents, and we knew it. Cinderella-ish took Shilling by the hand and led him to the front desk.

Outside, I ducked under some foliage along the tiki torch–lit pathway. Creeping toward the lagoon as stealthily as a wounded elephant seal, I grimaced with each step as my tender bare feet walked on landscape paved with sharp little stones. Just as I caught sight of the coin-filled pond, a frightened gecko skittered across the top of my right foot. I covered my mouth to silence a girlish squeal.

Meanwhile, Cinderella was whispering something into the desk clerk's ear. It was obviously of great importance, as Shilling watched the clerk's eyes widen. A lost kid was a high priority at this resort. The desk clerk regained his composure and said in a sickly-sweet voice, "Don't worry, kid. I'll find your parents in a jiffy. Do you know what room they are in?"

Shilling shook his head mutely. The dumber he acted, the better. He turned his head and focused on all the light switches against the back wall—especially the third one to the left on the second panel, which was labeled "koi pond lights."

I sat by the water's edge and pulled two pillowcases from my trousers. The fancy stitching on the linen read, *May all your dreams come true.* Even at age ten, I could appreciate the irony of that. I gazed upward at the busy bridge and watched as a few pennies flew down from the sky. They created small ripples in the aqua-blue pond and drifted past the koi, landing ever so gently on the bottom of the pool. The yellow and green underwater lights enhanced all the copper and silver, creating an image of a genuine sunken treasure. Walt could not have drawn anything more magical. God, I already loved this place.

At the front desk, it was now or never. Shilling took a deep breath and wandered around the oversized counter to the wall of light switches. He turned off the koi pond switch and then took off like a bolt of lightning, leaving the Cinderella and the hotel clerk looking concerned.

The lights were out, and that was the cue. Hastily I took off my shirt, pants, and underwear and slid along the algae-covered concrete into the chilly water.

Just above me, Shilling ran across the bridge and tore down the pathway to the bounty that lay below. Along the way he also discarded every item of clothing he was wearing. We were smart enough to know if we both came back to the hotel room sopping wet, Mr. and Mrs. Shilling would know what was what. I had already put four quarters, three dimes, and six pennies into his pillowcase when Shilling tapped my back. I smiled and handed him his pillowcase. "There's ton of pennies down there. Must be a lot of cheap dorks staying here," I complained.

"No pennies," Shilling replied. "Just the good stuff."

The water wasn't that deep, reaching just past our knees. And in the Florida weather, the cool water felt great. As I scooped more money into my pillowcase, I couldn't help but giggle and think I was having the vacation of a lifetime—and we hadn't even been into Disney World yet.

"Holy moly. I think I just stepped on a half dollar. I can feel it with my big toe," I said. I plunged downward…or as down as I could get in two feet of water. My bare behind popped up in the moonlight. Shilling giggled and thought that if someone looked down from the bridge right then, they'd assume Disney had imported some exotic pink jellyfish.

According to our plan, the koi would huddle over at one end of the pond like sheep as the new guys in the pond ran the roost. Not the case. Koi are notoriously feisty, mean, and fast. The first fish nibbled on Shilling's toes. He jerked in shock and dropped a fistful of coins. I heard the commotion and saw all the bubbles escaping from Shilling's mouth. Then I noticed that a giant gold koi hanging on to his toe like it was a human fishhook. Shilling was squirming something crazy.

I couldn't help but stand there laughing so hard I almost coughed up a lung.

The mighty sea beast finally released its grip, and Shilling looked at me angrily. "You coulda helped, dill weed."

"What? It's a giant goldfish." I was scientifically correct.

"OK, keep going." Shilling dived back under.

For the next three minutes, the money was rolling in. And the fish were tenacious, but we didn't care. All we could see was the candy, the Pirates of the Caribbean souvenirs, and the Tomorrowland pins in our pockets the next day at the park. I imagined we had enough to equal two years' worth of allowance. We both wondered how we were going to hide all this change from his parents. But these were fleeting thoughts. Our adrenaline was at such a heightened state that pretty much all rational thinking was kaput.

Suddenly the lights came back on, bright and harsh. Shilling and I immediately closed our eyes due to the sheer wattage of the underwater glare. From the bridge above, the scene must have been something to behold. Two bare-naked boys frolicking in a pond with pillowcases full of poached coins that had been tossed with good intentions and trust. Shilling and I raised our heads above the water and realized we were onstage. People were looking down. Some were even waving their fists in anger. We quickly lowered our bags to cover our privates.

A woman told her daughter, "Oh, honey, look away. This is disgraceful. Where are those boys' parents?"

"Somebody call the police!" another man said.

A teenager had a less serious accusation: "Hey! We see your little Pinocchio peckers." This was followed by a roar of laughter.

"Foxton, take your bag and run like heck!" Shilling said.

We sprang out of the pool, ignoring the sharp little stones, and ran back up the pathway. We dashed, buck naked, through the corridors of the Polynesian Hotel. Everyone we encountered moved out of our way as if we had leprosy. Shilling and I tried to hide our genitalia with pillowcases jingling with coins. So we kept switching the bags in front of and then behind ourselves in sheer panic.

Finally we reached our room and let out a joint sigh of relief. Shilling suddenly became still. "The room keys are in my pants," he said.

"So is my wallet with my school ID card," I said, gulping.

Defeat washed over us. Shilling lowered his head and surrendered to the reality of the situation. He knocked and then looked at me as if he were a prisoner on his way to the gallows. Mrs. Shilling opened the door and gasped. Mr. Shilling was on the bed and opened his mouth, appearing much like the koi we'd just encountered. There stood two stooges at the doorway: dripping wet, naked, and holding stolen goods.

The door closed in my face, and I was left in the hallway in my birthday suit. Legend has it when that door closed, Shilling suffered more than a few harsh words. Mrs. Shilling actually walked back to the hotel restaurant's kitchen and borrowed a wooden spoon from a mystified chef. Twenty minutes later she returned with that same spoon, now broken in half.

Later that evening, when he could actually walk and I could put on clothes, Shilling and I headed in shame to the front desk and apologized for everything. Cinderella actually gave us a kiss on the forehead for being so honest.

That night went down in infamy with the rest of the boys on West Ambler Road. Heroes. Pure and simple. Shilling and I also realized that, despite everything, we'd walked away with something more precious than money: a lifelong memory that would be told over and over in great detail to many an enraptured listener. The next day we had almost as much fun in Disney World as one could imagine.

If only Melissa were here with me, holding my hand, I thought. My obsession had begun.

Barbie, Ken, and the Angry Mob

Coming home on the plane, I thought of nothing but Melissa and goofing around with Hurl. In the mind of a ten-year-old, four days away is a long, long time. I knew I'd just have to wait for the right moment with Melissa, but Hurl would be up for anything. And what I had in mind was the complete destruction of an entire village.

On the left side of the Hirlingtons' unruly lawn was a twelve-foot-deep trench that ran parallel from the front of the house all the way back and beyond. If Hurl's lawn was a "cesspool," then the ravine and the tinkling stream at the bottom were the Amazon. We had found tadpoles bigger than our pinkie fingers and toads louder than Mrs. Munson's car. Heck, we'd had to use old man Hirlington's rarely used golf clubs as machetes to even get down there.

Hurl and I had found the best time to explore the Wild Kingdom was after it rained, and it had been pouring since late the night before. The only catch was we had to get permission from his overprotective mom. And today, judging by all the cars parked at his house, Mrs. Hirlington was having one of her ladies' card games—a big feather in our cap, because she rarely paid attention to what Hurl had to say on card day. Especially if she was winning. So we usually stood at the top of the stairs until the excitement heated up in the game. Unbeknownst to most of them (who were soused anyway), we'd run down the stairs like boys on fire. "Going to the ravine," we said so fast it was basically another language.

Mrs. Hirlington and her friends looked at us, confused from our statement and probably from all the Harvey Wallbangers they were drinking. It was a perfect storm for getting away with murder.

Today was no different. We walked into the house, and the cigarette smoke was thick as shaving cream. Somebody must be losing bad.

Mrs. Hirlington barely looked up from her cards. "Hello, Bun Bun."

Hurl cringed. "Mom, I told you not to call me that anymore. Like five years ago."

Mrs. Hirlington said, "I know, dear, but the ladies all have names for their kids. Right, Doe?"

Doe sat next to Mrs. Hirlington and was named appropriately. She was wide-eyed and particularly stupid looking. We could never figure out whether she was a genius or a human mannequin. Doe would occasionally spurt out every answer to the questions on *Jeopardy* and ten minutes later would say, "I have a sister. She's my mom's daughter, you know. Anyway, the other day we went to that new mall..." At the table, Doe shouted out, "I still call my girl Curlicue."

Across the table Estelle Jensen pointed out that her two boys were "Goofus and Gallant. And we all know who Goofus is." The ladies all laughed. We knew who Goofus was too. Poor Rich Jensen—ten years old and already pegged as a buffoon.

Hurl shrugged. He'd actually given up on the Bun Bun thing years ago.

I, on the other hand, had no name like that in my house except when I got into trouble—meathead, birdbrain, and soft skull were a few. I'd never tell Hurl, but I'd have taken just about any name over Bun Bun.

We went upstairs and devised our plan to get down to the Wild Kingdom. I pulled out some random toy and start playing loudly while Hurl did some spy work at the top of the stairs. "No big pots yet," he whispered.

Sometimes there was a mound of coins two inches deep in the middle of that card table. Once Hurl said he'd seen a watch in the pile. These ladies were not casual gamblers. And most of the time, we learned new swear words just from listening to them yak.

For the past twenty minutes, I'd had Hurl's G.I. Joe riding in the Johnny Quest cruiser and pretending to swim with Aquaman. I took Hurl's flashlight and tried to interrogate G.I. Joe. I threatened the plastic doll with a little fire, and he sang like a canary. But I was getting bored with G.I. Joe now. I'd never had a thing for soldiers…unless they were being attacked by giant bugs. Sometimes when my mom and dad weren't home, we'd pour lighter fluid on them, toss a match, and pretend they'd been hit with the flamethrower. Hurl did the best screams, so we let him be the burned soldier. I counted an entire regiment once—doomed to the horrors of a Kingsford charcoal lighter.

"C'mon…the water level will go down," I whined impatiently.

"Shhhh. I think it's getting serious," Hurl said. "They are getting quiet down there."

I had to get out for another reason: the smoke was smothering me. I didn't understand why grownups would do that. It smelled like crapola and burned my throat. I didn't think it looked cool until Debbie Rundberg told me it did seven years later. Then I picked up the nasty habit for a year.

"OK," Hurl said.

I threw traitorous Joe against the wall. I went over to Hurl, and I could feel the tension as each lady laid down a card.

Hurl said, "Three, two, one…last one is a tampon."

We hauled ass down the stairs, poorly enunciating our destination: "Goingtotheravinebye."

They didn't even know what had hit them. We just bolted out the screen door.

"Nice going, Bun Bun," I said.

Hurl punched me in the arm. And as soon as we got into the garage, we heard all the ladies erupt in excitement. Somebody had won big. I hoped it was Mrs. Hirlington. They needed money the most.

Mr. Hirlington's golf clubs were collecting dust, spiderwebs, and perhaps large species of rodents in the corner of the garage. Hurl got the big driver. I preferred a wedge myself—I'd found it cut through the overgrowth better.

"You think all the old stuff is down there?" asked Hurl, "Look at that place. Nobody has been in those weeds in two months."

I thought about that for a second. He said nothing. God only knew what we would find. Oh well. Who cared?

Before we even reached the edge of the drop-off, we had to cut through tall grass, prehistoric weeds, and even young trees. And the mugginess brought out the mosquitos.

Hurl held out his hand. "You got the OFF?"

Before coming over I'd taken a can from our garage. We both rubbed it on like suntan lotion, and the mosquitos let us alone. We gazed over the edge of the giant drop-off, wearing you-go, no-you-go faces.

I caved. "Fine, but I get to tell the story at the fence post."

Hurl was no fool. "Fine by me."

I edged my foot over the top of the hill and scoped out the route that would leave me with the fewest leg scratches later. Fear may be a great motivator, but my mom and her bottle of Bactine were worse. On the left were jagged rocks. To the right the path was just straight down. I seemed to remember we'd taken the center route the year before. It was full of prickly weeds and tree roots, but it seemed our best chance at avoiding death.

"Three, two, one…last one's a tampon," I said.

My descent wasn't graceful. It wasn't even slow or calculated. I just kind of flopped down there with dirt kicking up, my sneakers in front of me as my only protection and, as far as I could tell, a rip in my new shirt the only casualty. Made it. I looked up at Hurl, and he was shrewdly plotting his way, avoiding my mistakes and making it down in a somewhat smoother fashion.

We brushed ourselves off and surveyed the situation. The trickle of water was now a small flowing river. A little downstream we could see all our tools, and most of them looked intact.

We stepped into the water, getting our shoes wet. It was easier than chopping down all the flora and fauna on the sides. We got to the dam site and saw that the entire Barbie Village we'd ripped off from the Salvation Army Dumpster was still there. It was rotted and covered in weeds but still standing. The rocks we'd used to dam up the river were still there as well.

"We might need more rocks. The river is pretty high," Hurl said, as chief architect for our Barbie Village annihilation scenario.

We picked up as many rocks as we could and began piling them up one by one, making sure there were as few leaks in the dam as possible. Soon it was apparent we were going to need a better stoppage system. The water was so strong it was leaking around the sides. We began to gather sticks, weeds, and anything that would block the water. Hurl had the brilliant idea of using mud from the bottom of the creek to patch the holes, making the top of the dam as sturdy as she'd ever been. We looked at each other and wiped our filthy hands on our pants and shirts. We gazed lovingly at our construction, as proud as the men who'd built the Empire State Building.

But time was of the essence. Judging by the water level, we had about fifteen minutes to set up the peaceful little Barbie Village and all its unwitting inhabitants.

We took great care in assembling this. The castle had to be placed directly under the dam for maximum damage. We placed the three unclothed Barbies at the Barbie tea table to enjoy their refreshments. The idiot Ken doll was positioned on a chaise lounge, getting sun. Barbie's Jeep—check. Barbie's bed set—check. Now all we had to do was let Mother Nature rain down upon Barbieville and create the greatest catastrophe the world had ever seen.

This may or may not have prompted Hurl's philosophical question: "You think you go to heaven when you die?"

"Don't know. Haven't thought about it really," I said, lying. I had thought about it quite a bit since Tante had arrived.

"I mean, do you think there's a band up there playing in front of George Washington? Alice Cooper, maybe?"

"Alice Cooper is still alive. I saw his posters in New York."

Hurl thought for a moment. "OK, that fat lady who sings 'California Dreaming' on Ed Sullivan—she died."

"Yeah, she did. Maybe."

"I mean, we all go there, right? Doing something like this wouldn't put us in hell or anything?"

I giggled. "No, Hurl, killing plastic Barbies will not put us in hell."

Hurl wasn't giving up on the subject. "What about when we blow up minnows with firecrackers? God says every living thing is sacred."

For that I didn't have an answer.

The dam was almost reaching peak level.

"It won't be long now…ha ha," I said, ending the sentence like Blofeld from the Bond movies.

Hurl bent down on the Barbie side. "I like watching it from this angle. More destruction."

The water was brimming at the top, and small waves were escaping and starting to tickle Barbie's feet.

I did my best girl impression: "You feel that water, Barbie?"

Hurl raised his voice and said, "Oh yes, Barbie…we may have to go inside before it rains."

"Ken will save us," I said. But Ken lay there like a lump on a log. Useless.

The dam broke. Water gushed everywhere. The castle was the first to go, tipping over with ferocity. Barbie and her three friends crashed into some boulders and drowned within minutes, lying facedown in the water. We always saved Ken—the man who betrayed all men by being in the Barbie world in the first place—for last. His chaise lounge started floating down the river. Uncontrollably. We could hear him scream like a little girl. Served him right.

This was the greatest flood ever until it hit.

It fell with not so much a thud but a cloud of white dust and a musty smell. Luckily it dropped right from the sky between us. Neither Hurl nor I could make out anything for a few moments until we wiped the ash from our eyes. Then we heard it: a low rumbling at first. A humming that was rhythmic but also a buzzing that sounded angry. Both of us looked where the thing dropped and then looked upward. It was gone—the giant wasp nest that used to be above us had been growing like a tumor every year since we'd been able to play outside by ourselves.

The first sting was like a gentle pinprick—nothing more than a minor nuisance, actually.

Hurl and I were stung in the face at once: me on my cheek and Hurl on his forehead.

I am not sure who screamed like the Ken doll first. The hive on the ground was half-submerged in water and twice the size of a watermelon. Whatever had made that home for thousands of wasps fall from its tree branch was our doing in the collective mind of the thousands of angry insects. The moment they started climbing up into our shirts, Hurl and I scrambled up that hill.

We had wet sneakers and a furious horde on our tails. This was more like something that would happen to Scooby Doo and Shaggy than to two real live boys. We made it to the top and by then must have been stung twenty times with many more to come. I didn't even look at Hurl as he made his way into his house. I think I heard all the ladies cry in terror after the door slammed, but I really don't know. Self-preservation is a strange thing. When you are running for your life, nothing else exists in the world.

I can only imagine what it looked like to the foreign eye: a small boy with ripped clothes, many bloodstains from cuts and bruises, and a black cloud of angry venom following him with a vengeance.

I opened our front door, shrieking, "Mom! Mom! Wasps! I got wasps everywhere!"

My mom rounded the corner from the kitchen and dropped our family's dinner on the floor. She waved as many wasps as she could away from herself, took me by the collar, and basically threw me into the shower. She turned the faucet on full blast and slammed the door. I peeled off my wasp-infested clothes, and the shower water seemed to have some effect, as they were getting soaked and began floating down the drain.

Needless to say, Mom's first concern was *not* my safety. She was pissed. "What did you do?" she hissed. "I told you never to play around near those nests."

"It just fell, Mom—I swear. We were down by the Hirlingtons' creek, and the whole thing crashed into the ground by our feet." At this point I didn't even feel the stings anymore…except the ones down below. There had been bees between my butt cheeks. It was like they knew where it hurt the most.

Soon they were all gone. Down the drain. Or dead on the floor.

"We have to go to the doctor, but first I just want you to soak in the tub. Cold water, mister!" Mom said.

I was pretty sure the cold water was for punishment and not some medical remedy. I heard Mom run out the door, saying, "Shooo!" over and over. Then I heard her spraying some insecticide. I lay there, crying now and getting sorer by the minute. I was not allergic to wasps, and neither was Hurl, so we ended up OK—except we looked like a couple of young men with really bad acne for a day or two. And I walked kind of funny. But that story the next night was a major hit on the fence post, equaling the laughs from the koi pond.

And as I lay there in the tub, I couldn't help thinking, *What if that Barbie Village were real? And those Barbie dolls and Ken were real too. And the wasps were giant atomic mutations. Man, that would have been really cool.*

The Mummy's Hand

IT WAS A DREAM COME true. That Saturday night they were showing the superior *The Mummy's Hand*, which featured Dick Foran as the stalwart hero, George Zucco as the devious high priest, and Tom Tyler as the mummy. As far as old Universal mummy pictures go, this was the best. The original *Mummy* featured Boris Karloff as the monster in full makeup for the first five minutes; then he transforms into an old man mumbling ancient things for the next hour and a half. As a kid, I thought it was boring. It was very clear I was a monster nerd. Ask me the capital of North Dakota. Huh? Ask me who played Renfield in *Dracula*, and I could tell you it was Dwight Frye in a heartbeat.

Jeremy and I sat cross-legged on the floor with a pan of Jiffy Pop between us. The commercial ended for Virginia Slims, and the movie began with the Universal logo. Then came the title sequence with the old Hollywood music. Immediately we were swept up in a time and place that existed only in our dreams: Cairo. Thievery. Bravery. A pretty girl. And the great threat of an inhuman, walking, million-year-old man wrapped in bandages primed to choke the intruders to his tomb. My heart beat faster. I was not on West Ambler Road anymore; I was across the Atlantic Ocean in Africa. All my problems, fears, and worries drifted far away for the next ninety minutes. It was me, a handful of popcorn, Jeremy, and the forces of evil.

Jeremy liked these movies, but he was certainly not obsessed like me. I couldn't really blame him. Back then monster fans were few and far between. I had to hide my magazines when I bought them in the magazine store for fear of ridicule. To the rest of the world, this kind of stuff meant you were not right in the head. Rarely could I ever find another to talk to about horror movies, makeup, and special effects.

On TV, *The Mummy's Hand* wasted no time getting to the good stuff. We didn't even see the hero for the first ten minutes. Until then, it was all mummy and evil plans. A new, creepy-looking high priest went to this old tomb to find the grand guru of old priests. He was sitting in this ancient room filled with steam and Egyptian artifacts.

The new creepy guy said, "I have answered your summons, my high priest."

Now the old guy was about to kick the bucket, but he had one last task: "It's good you arrived by sunset. I shall not see the moon sink beyond the valley of the jackals again."

Then there were a bunch of flashbacks to ancient Egypt, where this dude, Kharis, loves this princess, Anaka.

Here's his spiel: "I must hand over to you the secrets of the priests from the high gods of Karnak. Two thousand years ago, Anaka died. She was burned with all the ceremony of her exalted status. Kharis, prince of the royal house, loved Anaka, so after her burial, he broke into the altar room of Isis to steal the secret of eternal life. With that he could bring Anaka back to life, daring the anger of the ancient gods with the forbidden tana leaves. For the sin he had committed, Kharis was condemned to be buried alive. But first they cut out his tongue (awesome part) so the gods would not be assailed by his unholy curses."

"Kharis was buried alone and with him a large quantity of tana leaves. For over three thousand years, Kharis has remained in his cave on the other side of this mountain to bring death to whoever defiled Anaka's tomb, for Kharis *never really died*." The first time I heard that, it scared the pee out of me. *Never really died.* Oh boy.

Then there was some other gobbeldygook about resurrecting the mummy. The old guy sputtered, "Under the idol of Isis, you will find a copper box. In this box lies the secret to life. Tana leaves. The food for the mummy." And that was all in the first five minutes.

The old guy still rambled on, "Three of the leaves will make enough fluid to keep Kharis's heart beating. Burn three tana leaves, and give the fluid to Kharis." Then some wolves howled, and the old man even quoted Dracula: "Listen to the children of the night." He continued, "Kharis must be fed. Should unbelievers desecrate the tomb of Anaka, you will use *nine* tana leaves each night to give life and movement to Kharis, and thus you will enable him to bring vengeance on the heads of those who enter. Should Kharis retain the fluid of more than nine tana leaves, he will become an uncontrollable monster demon with a desire to kill and kill."

Plot understood. And already scary. Then came a commercial for shampoo. Time to get more salt for the popcorn and a Fireball.

The movie got underway again, and a mix of chemical Fireball and popcorn assaulted my taste buds. As was customary, Jeremy gripped a pillow like a life preserver, holding it close to his chest in case of a heart attack.

The hero and his traveling sidekick got involved in some convoluted mess with a magician and his daughter, and off they went to the mummy's tomb, which resulted in ten to fifteen minutes of boring archeological digging until they find the tomb. This was when I switched over to channel eleven, which was broadcasting Chiller Theatre. I got up to turn the unwieldy knob on our RCA Victor color set.

"Jim!" Jeremy yelled, transfixed.

Now, as a ten-year-old, I was entitled to certain things with my younger brother. Number one was that whatever I said went. Number two was I could occasionally be a selfish jerk. Number three was, of course, the *I'll tell Mom* threat. Never failed.

Jeremy was clearly perturbed I was turning to channel eleven. The Chiller Theatre features were usually lowbrow stuff, but occasionally we got lucky. But not that night. It was a crappy thing called *Dungeons of Harrow*, and it was just awful.

"I just wanted to see, pinhead," I snapped at Jeremy.

I switched back to channel five with a thunderous click every time I turned the channel.

The characters were still digging for Anaka's tomb. *C'mon.* Jeremy went stiff again, just waiting for our bandaged friend to make his grand entrance.

In the hallway I saw Tante walking by very slowly. Usually at this time of night, she was bouncing around, baking, and playing with us boys on our bicycles. But Tante was different now. My mom said this was what happened when people got old. "Down here," she'd said, pointing to her stomach. "And up here." She had pointed to her head. I didn't understand that, and more importantly, I didn't *want* to understand that. This was Tante, the coolest and wisest old person ever—and that includes Batman's butler, Alfred. Tante looked cold, and she was covered in a blanket. Maybe it was just me, but she didn't really look like she knew what to do or where to go.

"Tante, come watch *The Mummy* with us."

"Yeah, Tante, it's scaaaarrrry," Jeremy added, the pillow closer to his eyes than ever.

Tante looked at us from the darkened hallway. "Chim, Cheremy, this house is full of books. Go read *Wuthering Heights*," she said, wearing a scowl that was never a real scowl but just a play face when she tried to be serious.

"C'mon, Tante, he's almost here," I begged.

"Who's almost here?" Tante was as lucid as ever. "The creature with the wasp stings all over his face?"

Jeremy and I clarified in unison, "The mummy!"

"Oh, all right. The things Tante does for her grandsons. You both now owe me an hour of weeding in the garden."

Jeremy and I smiled. We had heard this before, and it meant more playing with the hose while Tante bent over and picked weeds. We also knew Tante would not be doing much weeding anymore. That time looked like it was closing in fast.

Tante slowly walked into our domain and took a seat on the couch behind us. When she sat, we heard a very loud sigh, as if someone had just taken a fifty-pound weight off her shoulders. "OK, what's going on in this nonsense?" she demanded in her Tante way.

I explained the very thin plot to her, and she mumbled something again about *Wuthering Heights* being a brilliant story. What the heck was *Wuthering Heights*?

Finally the band of questionable archeologists entered the tomb of Anaka. As usual, like in *Star Trek*, they had one disposable guy to be killed first.

The mummy made his appearance, and this was where it got really scary—with dirty five-thousand-year-old bandages, one arm still taped to his side, and one menacing hand groping for throats to choke. And for some reason, in this movie, they made his eyes pitch-black, like there was nothing behind that rotting cloth. It was terrifying. I was grinning and giggling like a schoolgirl.

Even Tante gasped when Kharis (the mummy) choked his first victim with no remorse. "I think your grandfather took me to see this," she said. "He loved these kind of movies, you know."

What was this? My grandpa, who I barely remembered from before he died of cancer, had liked monster movies? It was in my genes. This would explain much.

Tante continued. Jeremy kept watching the mummy wreak havoc as all my attention went to the only woman I truly had learned to love up to that point in my life.

"I always wanted to go to the Bogart and Ronald Coleman pictures, and your grandpa made a deal with me—sly one, he was." She smiled fondly.

I was all ears.

"We switched back and forth. *Gone with the Wind* meant *King Kong* the following week. *Casablanca* meant *The Wolfman*. It went on like that until—" She stopped talking at that point.

"So you saw all these movies I watch every Saturday night?"

"Almost."

"Why didn't you tell me? I thought you hated these things." I had never been more interested in my family history.

"I do. But I loved your grandpa so much I would do it for him. Just like he would go see a love story for me. That's what people do when they are in love. They make sacrifices. Even if they are as silly as monster movies. These movies remind me of him. Sometimes they are hard to watch. One day you will understand."

"So if Grandpa loved monster movies, you must think I maybe have a little of Grandpa still in me?"

"Oh yes, I see it as clear as day—even in this dark room. Your eyes. Your wit. Your lack of patience."

"What?"

"Oh yes, your grandpa was, shall we say, a little bit of a baby if he didn't get his way. Just like you when one of your fireworks doesn't go off. The stomping. And the pouting. And the whining." She laughed.

I was smiling too.

"We don't talk a lot about the ones we lost. Maybe it's just your grandma, but you should know more. Like you, he loved the beach, cookouts, and bratwurst...and his beer. You don't want to like beer, Chim. You don't want a beer belly like him." Tante extended her hand from her stomach by a foot. "All the baking too—I didn't help much with the belly. Anyway, he had a bicycle like you when he was a boy in Germany. He told me he used to ride it in the mountains for hours."

"You didn't meet Grandpa until you came here, right?"

"Yes, Chim. We met at a dance. When he held out his hand and asked me to dance, his hand was shaking. He was so handsome. Just like you."

Meanwhile, back in Mummy-land, the creature was now out of control and starting to kill off the cast one by one. I looked back at Jeremy. He was petrified and loving every second of it. And I would have joined him of course, but this was more interesting than a Universal monster. That's how important it was.

Tante also looked at Jeremy. "You both remind me of him. Jeremy has your grandfather's sweetness."

I looked at him and laughed.

"Shut up, wiener brain," he said.

Tante ignored the comment. "Oh no, Chim—you are sweet too, but Cheremy and your grandpa had an inner innocence to them. You are an old soul, Chim. They were brand-new."

"Brand-new to what?"

"This world. I believe you come back when you die as something else on this earth. God recycles you. Uses you for something else in his world."

"You mean, Grandpa could be like a raccoon?"

"He liked raccoons. I am sure your grandpa would be very happy in a tree all day."

I pondered that for a moment. "So with a little luck, I could come back as the creature from the Black Lagoon?"

Tante smiled. "There's the wit I was talking about."

"Tante, do you think I'm a good person? I don't mean being polite or anything but a good person."

She was taken aback. "Come here." She patted the couch next to her.

I slowly got up, and she put her wafer-thin arms around me. "Of course you're a good person. Why do you ask such a thing?"

"I don't know...'cause I like monsters. Getting into trouble. Riding my bike where I'm not supposed to go. And I've stolen a few candy bars from Borchette's." It all came pouring out.

"Stealing candy bars is not a good thing. And I want you to repay that man as soon as you can, Chim."

I was ashamed.

"Everything else is just being a human being. Especially a little one. Well, you aren't so little anymore, are you?"

She hugged me, and I hugged her back.

"I guess not. And I'm not sure I want to grow any older. I like where I am now. My bike, my comics, and my games. I see what it's like with older kids. Hanging around. Doing nothing. Looks boring. I want to stay just like this right here. And summer forever."

"I don't blame you. But getting old is also exciting. Soon you will be liking the girls, yes?" Tante saw something gleam in my eye. "You like the girls now. A particular girl?"

My face turned a deep shade of red and my head resembled a rubber playground ball.

Tante looked very surprised. "A particular girl."

"Nah, it's nothing," I blurted out as fast as I could.

Tante, knowing better than to push it, said, "I see. OK."

I put my head on Tante's shoulder. And for the first time in my life, I fell asleep during a monster movie. Before I closed my eyes and conked out, I thought I heard her say, "Maybe you'll find a girl who likes monsters someday."

She (Part 2)

There were no McDonald's in Westport at that time. There was Caroll's, a fast-food grease palace that was *the* place to be seen during the school year. Just like McDonald's, it was quick and relatively decent, and it had crispy fries that were unmatched.

Two days after the great insect attack, my dad decided my facial appearance had now gone from a radioactive chicken pox look to just bad acne. I still had red marks all over my face, but the swelling had gone down. Dad took me, Shilling, Jeremy, and Hurl (who looked worse than I did). Every time Shilling looked our way, he sang the Clearasil jingle: "*Pow! Pow! Get the powerful Clearasil Power.*" This got a laugh from Dad and Jeremy. Hurl and I felt like idiots. But being cooped up in our rooms for forty-eight hours and the temptation of a Caroll's club burger made the risk of being seen in public seem worth it.

"So what are your plans for the rest of the summer, boys?" Dad asked as if we were in a job interview.

We all looked at one another in a clueless Moe-Larry-Curly fashion.

He was chomping away on his burger. "Well, you gotta have something planned. Mowing a lawn or two? Going to the beach? We're almost in August. You know, you could help Tante out a lot by doing some yard work."

Question to the universe: Why do dads always have to make you feel guilty about something?

Could be the smallest detail, but there is always some sort of hassle attached: "Jimmy, if you're gonna stay up and watch monster movies, you gotta get up and get that garage cleaned out." Or "Jimmy, carpets don't clean themselves; please pick up that clump of dirt."

Someone had to answer his question. "I don't know, Dad."

Shilling responded, making us all look very bad, "I am thinking about taking a part-time job washing dishes, Mr. Foxton."

"Well, you're a little young for such a thing. I didn't mean a *job* job." Dad swallowed half a pound of meat.

"It's OK, Mr. Foxton. My dad knows the guy at the Chinese restaurant."

My dad rolled his eyes. "Yes, I know him too. He's going to hire you?"

"Just a few nights a week, Mr. Foxton."

Shilling's dead-on Eddie Haskell impression was getting on our nerves. My attention was drawn to the back of the restaurant, where a bunch of girls were giggling. Loudly. One of them was Melissa Praddleton. My heart skipped a beat before I thought about my face. My god.

I had turned into the thing I loved the most: a monster.

I noticed most of us were finished, and it was customary for Dad to take us just down the street after Carrol's for an ice cream cone at Carvel. I began gathering everyone's burger wrappers, straws, and empty soda cups.

"Who's up for a cone?" Dad did not need to ask.

We all raised our hands just as another burst of giggling broke out from the girls in the back.

We were sitting near the door, so it was easy to make a quick escape. I dumped all the trash in the bin, made it to safety outside, and attempted a little jog to the car.

"Somebody wants a chocolate-dipped cone!" Dad called out as everybody exited the restaurant.

We piled into the Impala and drove down the street.

Dad was very proud of his new Chevy. He wanted nothing more than to pull up to the ice cream stand and walk out like a big shot, but it was not to be. The place was mobbed. The line for the single window was twenty deep. My dad took a deep breath of pure disappointment and parked in the back.

We got in line. The wait wasn't going to be long; besides, it would take us a while to decide on what we wanted.

I knew, of course: a vanilla cone dipped in chocolate that somehow froze and became a hard shell. It was a miracle of culinary science. Dad knew exactly what I wanted, and it was a great way to finish off the night.

Until I heard the giggling again. This time behind me. I dared not turn my head, but my suspicion was Melissa and her friends were about five people behind us.

Shilling said, "What are you getting, Foxton?"

"Chocolate-dipped vanilla," I mumbled.

"What?" Shilling said, confused.

"Doesn't matter," I mumbled again. I was minutes from Melissa seeing my hideousness.

A second window opened for business, and the gang of girls made a run for it, frustrating my father to no end. There were six girls in all. All in cheerleader garb. Including Melissa. They were ordering furiously, and we were inching closer to our window a.k.a. my doom.

Maybe I'll be OK, I thought. Those girls were laughing up a storm and nothing mattered to them anyway. They were in their own world. Probably talking about the football players, Donny Osmond, or Burt Reynolds.

The five of us got to our window and began to order. I was the last one.

Quietly I said, "A vanilla cone dipped in chocolate."

The lady behind the window said quite loudly, "Speak up, honey. I can't hear you."

That's when the cheerleaders turned their attention upon my appearance.

One said, "Ewwwwww."

Another said, "Try rubbing alcohol."

Hurl looked at me sympathetically. "Don't even listen to them. Their team stinks anyway."

Shilling was even more protective. "Try a new face." Whatever that meant.

Melissa recognized me immediately and did not say a word. Or make a face. She was silent.

None of them would ever have known she knew me. I didn't blame her.

The girls all got served and went around to the left-hand side of the ice cream stand, where the picnic tables were. Giggling ensued.

We got our cones and followed them. Five of the girls were at the table, and Melissa was at the back of the restaurant, unwrapping her ice cream sandwich. My dad chose a table far away, and everybody sat down except for me.

"I gotta get some napkins," I said, heading to the front of the restaurant. When I got there, I ran around the other side to the back, where Melissa was still unwrapping her treat. "Hey, Melissa," I said.

She looked at me, confused. I'd guessed wrong. She didn't know me at all.

"It's me, Jimmy. From the other day. At Saint Luke's."

"Oh yeah." She smiled.

"I just came to tell you I am sorry about this." I pointed to my face.

"Sorry about what?" Again, she was confused.

"My face."

"Oh, I've seen much worse. It'll go away."

"No, you don't understand. These are wasp stings. I was attacked by a wasps."

Melissa laughed so hard she dropped her ice cream sandwich. "Oh crud."

"We can share mine." I gave her the first bite.

"I really just thought you had a lot of zits." She was still laughing as she licked my cone. "I'm sorry...that must have hurt."

"Still does kinda."

"What did you do?"

"Hurl, my friend—you met him too at Saint Luke's—we were hanging out, and a wasp nest fell from a tree, and we just got stung. A lot."

"You could have died."

"Neither one of us was allergic." My gut was telling me to change the subject. Quickly. "What are you doing here? Cheerleading practice?" My powers of deduction were rather lame.

She handed me the cone. "Tonight was our first practice. Then we decided on a burger and a movie."

Great, I thought. *Movies*. Now we were in my arena. I took a bite out of the cone and handed it back to her.

"Butterflies Are Free."

"Oh," I said, knowing nothing about *Butterflies Are Free* except I wanted to be as far away as possible from it. But if she asked, I would see it. Immediately.

"Well, I guess I gotta get back to the gang." She took one more bite from my cone.

"OK. Thanks for understanding," I said.

"About what?" Once again, she was confused.

"My face."

She gave me a smile worth a million vanilla-dipped cones. "See you around, Jimmy Foxton."

"OK," I said. As she turned around, I ran back to the front of the store. I grabbed some napkins and brought them back to my gang, wheezing.

"About time," Shilling complained.

"I agree," said my dad as he grabbed a handful and wiped away half of Jeremy's cone, which had dripped on his shirt and the table.

I finished my cone in silence.

I'll see you around, indeed.

Melee's Bath

THE NEXT NIGHT AT THE fence post, Shilling blurted out he indeed was going to work at the Chinese restaurant next to his dad's new building. We were all stunned. No one had thought his proclamation at Carrol's was real. The legal working age in Connecticut was sixteen. Shilling was only ten, but he looked fifteen; however, in a kitchen of the questionable quality of the Golden Dragon, you could probably start washing dishes as soon as you learned to walk.

Mr. Melee, the owner, had made a fortune by owning one of the only Chinese restaurants in the area for decades. When I walked into the Golden Dragon, my first instinct was to notice that everything, and I mean everything, was gold. Soft gold chairs. Soft gold carpet. Gold plates and napkins. Even a golden painted aquarium that was home to a lobster that had been lying there forever.

The second thing I noticed was always Melee's pockmarked face and yellow-toothed smile. He was a slimy figure to rival Peter Lorre at his weaselly best. Often he would come around during the meal and say things to my dad like, "AhhhmrralpsIsheeyouwikegarlicfwiednoodle." There was no grammatical pause, no breath of air, no chance for your brain to digest anything Melee said. It was English, but it was English with no breaks. He stared back at my dad like some pinball machine waiting for a coin. Dad was a smart man but had no clue as to this new form of speed language. You would think after so many years in our town, Melee would know how to speak perfect English. My mom said it was because he wanted his restaurant to be authentic.

Then he'd creep around again and say, "IshdereanythingIcandoweasewet-thewaitwessknow."

For all we knew, Melee could have said he was going put my brother in a wok. Dad was now a little uncomfortable at the overextended two-sentence visit. It was clear boundaries were now being crossed. Melee took the hint and left with a ventriloquist's dummy's smile. As he turned I thought I saw him scowl. How in the world could Shilling's dad let him work in such a place?

Back at the fence post, Shilling confessed, "I gotta pay back for the lawn mower somehow."

We left it at that and felt sorry he had to spend the summer working.

A few nights later, Shilling came back to the nightly gathering and said working at the Golden Dragon was the coolest thing he'd ever done. He also said, "Foxton, Melee needs a bathroom attendant. I told him you would do it. He said be there tomorrow at four thirty."

"Whaaaa?"

"You don't make as much, but if you change the urinal cakes, wipe the toilets, and stuff, you'll get tips. By fall you'll have enough to buy whatever you want. Besides I saw your mom earlier and told her."

Heck, I didn't even wipe my own toilet. You think I'm gonna do it for some guy who just ate a pound of steamed eel? Besides I was only ten, and I looked like I was only ten. No way.

But it was too late: Shilling had told Mom.

When I got home later, she said, "A job will do you good."

"Ugh. Do I have to? Can't I do chores instead?" I begged like a man on death row.

"Maybe you can save enough for college."

Really? What kid thinks of saving for college? I wanted to save for something much more meaningful...like a minibike. So I caved, and Mom made me show up at the Golden Dragon a half hour early the next afternoon. Minibike or not, I was angry at Shilling and especially at my mom. I got out of the car and made my way slowly across the parking lot, looking toward the restaurant. Mom waved and honked. My thoughts turned to Sunday school, where we had recently learned about Judas.

The Golden Dragon used to be in the dumpy part of town, where all the gas stations and run-down stores were. But the restaurant had become so popular Melee had moved it into an abandoned fancy French restaurant that used to be called Le Meridian. Out front of the old Le Meridian restaurant was a huge fountain. On both sides of the massive stone structure, creepy cherubs peed water into a giant marble bowl. Lights flashed under the water, and King Neptune's head stuck out of the middle. He pointed a trident toward the sky. It was a ghastly thing. When the great water display had first been built, people would plan evenings around it, coming to watch while a happy crowd dined inside. Worst of all, unlike the hotel at Disney World, no one threw coins in the putrid water.

Huge windows showed off the aquatic scene to the diners. But the restaurant had failed, and now it was the Golden Dragon. The marquee above the door was written in Chinese lettering, but very clearly underneath that, you could easily see in red type calling it "Le Meridian." The Golden Dragon had to be the only Asian restaurant in the world to be adorned by a European fountain.

I opened the door, and there was Melee, smiling like a Cheshire cat. "Go back to the kitchen," he said in perfect English. Melee took me through the kitchen, where I was greeted with assorted grunts and looks of disdain. Immediately I thought of a prison. Shilling was off that night, and the dishwasher was none other than Renn Pickty. Renn and his brother, Harlan, were the most feared and loathsome characters in town. In any town, actually. An entire family built on the foundation of petty crime. Renn smiled with his rotten front tooth and gave me a big fat middle finger.

This simple threat was enough to possibly warrant a defibrillator, so I was glad to get right to polishing toilets. Melee walked me to the restroom. It was nice for a bathroom, I guess. Covered in marble. No graffiti. Everything was clean. Three stalls. Four sinks. Two urinals. Three paintings of Chinese acrobats. Melee told me my station was over by the sink. There before me were cloth towels, combs, Listerine, and a small bottle of cologne. "This is where you will stay, Foxton." Again he spoke perfectly.

"Understood."

"All night," he said, and then he added more salt to the wound. "You will ask the customer if they want a comb or some cologne. Then you will always give them a towel to wipe their hands. Then you will place the used towel in this bucket. Capisce?"

Capisce? Again with the Asian-European fusion thing.

He left me in my new chamber of horrors. Every move resounded in an echo, even the squeak of my sneakers. I waited for ten minutes. There was nothing to do but check myself out in the mirror. Oh my gosh, how in the world would Melissa Praddleton fall for this face?

The door opened, and the first gentleman walked in. He nodded and went into stall number three.

I could hear him wrestle with his belt. He sat, and his pants hit the floor. I turned away, embarrassed that I had been looking. Then he started talking to me. "Hey, boy, you have any Paco Rabon out there?"

I looked around. "I don't know what that is, sir."

"OK. Never mind. How about a newspaper?" He then grunted something awful. I made an *eeeewww* face.

"No, sir. Just combs, towels, and some cologne."

He grunted again, and the echo in the room loudly announced something big had splashed in the toilet. "You follow the Yankees?" he said again in a half moan.

Why was this guy talking to me during one of the most private times in a person's life? I felt like running out of the room right there and then. He continued doing his business. Then the stall opened, and he walked over to the sink. I was horrified. He washed his hands and thanked me by leaving fifty cents in the empty jar next to the combs. Fifty cents! Well, maybe I could go through with this after all.

They came and went all night. Thankfully no one else talked to me that much, but they did leave change. Some cheapskates deposited only a nickel in my minibike fund. Others were putting in quarters like crazy. Cleaning toilets wasn't bad as long as you closed your eyes and covered your mouth and nose with a paper towel. Easy peasy. At the end of the night, I didn't know how much I had in the jar until Melee walked in. He smiled. Not warmly. He walked over to the tip jar and counted every penny.

"Sixteen dollars and seventy-five cents. Very good."

"Thank you, Mr. Melee."

"That's more than we allow unless you are going to forfeit your pay."

"I don't understand," I said, sensing a scam.

"We pay dollar fifty an hour, and you worked four hours. If you made less than six dollars, I would pay you. But since you made sixteen dollars and seventy-five cents, that is more. Get it?

No pay. Tips only."

"Yes, Mr. Melee," I said angrily.

"Good. Now the cleaning supplies are in the closet next door. I want this bathroom sparkling for tomorrow." It took me the better part of two hours to clean that room, mopping, scrubbing, and wiping down everything in sight. Grown men are slobs. At one point I thought I was going to cry, but I held it in. The guys at the fence post would have been proud. And come to think of it, I had some new tales for the guys. That was worth more than his one dollar and fifty cents an hour.

The next day I told Shilling how Mr. Melee had gypped me. He said Mr. Melee was an "asswipe." I almost doubled over laughing; I had never heard "asswipe" before. He said he'd gotten it from the cooks, who called Mr. Melee that whenever he left the kitchen after giving orders.

I said, "I thought you said you loved the job."

Shilling replied, "I did until he cut my pay in half because I was so slow. Going to take me forever to repay that Toro lawnmower."

Two nights later I went to work with Shilling. Mr. Melee eyed us like criminals as we entered the lavish dining room. Melee rushed over to us as if we were on fire. He was huffing. "Never come through front door. Bad for business. Customer see slobby help and lose appetite. Go—get back there to kitchen and toilet."

We trudged back to our separate refugee camps. I felt sorry for Shilling. I'd taken a good look at his dishwashing station when I had my tour of his prehistoric kitchen conditions. There was a gigantic sink. Above that sink was a hose that looked like a boa constrictor. Shilling had said the water coming out of that hose would burn his hands if he didn't wear industrial gloves. The dishes came fast and furious. He had to wash down every one and put them all on a large plastic tray, which would then be put on a conveyor belt and sent into a scalding-hot dishwasher. When they came out, he had to put all the dishes in their rightful places. That is, until the next batch came, and he did it all over again. Six hours of that. I'd take the guy taking a crap and talking about baseball any day of the week.

Mr. Melee paid him one dollar and seventy-five cents an hour. That would be OK, I guess, if Mr. Melee didn't come in all the time, yelling, "What are you doing moving so slow? I pay you good money!"

Sometimes Shilling would take a break and come into the bathroom, and we'd giggle about how Melee was such an "asswipe." He was mean. And he treated everyone except his customers with contempt and cruelty.

One night we came in through the front door by mistake and he told us, "Tonight you work for half pay. Walk through front door again, and you look for another job with no good recommendation from me. Understand? Little idiots."

We told our parents about the abuse, but they said it was the real world: listen to your boss. This was the exact same way they reacted when we complained about our teachers at school.

"Mr. Burgess called me a dolt."

Well, that's how teachers teach sometimes.

"Mrs. Whitney slapped me on the back of the head."

Well, perhaps you deserved it.

When it came to authoritarian figures, a kid didn't stand a chance. They were right. You were wrong. This was 1972.

Melee continued to harass, cheat, scold, and abuse us until we decided to do the one thing a kid can do almost better than anyone: extract revenge.

What the heck? School was only six weeks away, so we didn't have to work there much longer.

The planning of the crime took several nights at the fence post. Movies such as *The Great Escape* had taught us we'd better have a good plan that was detailed to the second. In hindsight, devising the caper might have been more fun than the misdeed itself. We all had watches that would be synced. We drew the layout of the restaurant on the ground with a stick, using rocks as markers for my bathroom and the kitchen. It was a precision operation that would require all our skill and cunning. We could never get caught if we ever wanted to watch TV again; therefore we were very careful to make sure Operation: Golden Dragon went perfectly—unlike the Disney World disaster.

On the night of the great scandal, Shilling and I came in through the back door. Everything was normal. Melee was yelling at us and smiling at all his customers. We had picked a Saturday night so the damage would be extra special, since there were so many patrons. Our little event was set to go off at eight sharp—prime time for diners in our town. The restaurant was packed. People were eating a lot, which meant they were crapping a lot. My Lysol spray can was a lifesaver that night.

While Melee was making his rounds and speaking without periods, commas, semicolons, question marks, or exclamation points, I was in the bathroom doing what no one was paid enough to do.

Shilling was engrossed in the unholy steam of that dreaded sink. My Johnny Quest watch told me it was 7:58. Go time. My task was to tear off a wad of toilet paper and stuff it in the toilet. I flushed. Nothing went down, as planned. There was a gurgling sound as if the porcelain thing were going to throw up. Water began to rise. At 7:59 Shilling picked up a crate of glasses and headed for the door to the dining room. No one in the kitchen seemed to care. I exited the bathroom and found Melee. I told him we were going to have a flood. He excused himself and ran toward the bathroom. Shilling stood by the bathroom door with the glasses directly in Melee's path. They bumped, and Shilling dropped the entire tray of drinking glasses on the floor, creating a thunderous sound. At 8:00 on the dot, the entire restaurant looked up for what seemed like minutes. Melee was swearing, I think. And it was in Chinese.

At 8:01, Hurl and Jeremy were set in motion outside. In each of their hands were three giant boxes of Mr. Bubble soap. For the unenlightened, Mr.

Bubble was just as it sounds: a big pink box of soap that had a four-year-old kid frolicking in the suds on the front. No self-respecting ten-year-old would touch the stuff, but we'd gone into Shop and Stop and paid for it all with my tip money. At 8:02, Hurl and Jeremy already had the tops torn off the Mr. Bubble boxes. They ran up to the giant fountain in ski masks, dark clothing, and gloves in case the police took prints. Gleefully, they poured around 300 ounces of the cakey white power just under the peeing cherub.

At 8:03 Jeremy and Hurl ran across the street to a row of bushes to watch the disaster. Neither was seen by a soul. Everyone in the restaurant was still looking at the smashed dishes Shilling had dropped. Soon the excitement died down, and people began to start eating again. Melee grabbed my shirt collar like I was a bad dog. He dragged me into the bathroom, which was now an inch underwater. "Find me a plunger. Idiot."

Like most good things, our payback to Melee did not happen quickly. At 8:05, upon Melee's insistence, I reached into the toilet and grabbed the wadded-up toilet paper. Shilling was cleaning up the glass, using every ounce of self-control to not look out the window.

At 8:08, thirty yards away, an ominous bubble began to appear over the top of the great fountain outside the Golden Dragon. Melee had stopped chewing me out about the toilet. "Go get a mop," he barked and walked outside. As Melee passed Shilling, he fired him. Shilling gladly took off his dishwashing apron and went outside to join Hurl and Jeremy.

At 8:12 the diners started staring. Then they started pointing. Then they started laughing hysterically. Soon the entire place erupted. This thing in the fountain was now the size of a station wagon. Melee scurried over to the window, wondering what was so funny outside.

At 8:13 he gasped. And I saw his face. I'm still not exactly sure what came first. The protruding cartoon eyes. Or the mouth curled up so tightly you could actually see the outline of his teeth beneath the lips. He looked at me. I dropped the tip jar by his left foot and walked out the front door.

By 8:16 it was quite the spectacle. The suds were now towering eight feet above the rim of the fountain and continuing to grow. The peeing cherubs were no longer visible. The white foam kept rising like some huge amoeba.

By 8:17 no one had worked or eaten for fifteen minutes. Everyone was now at the window, gaping. First came the waiters. And then the kitchen staff. Traffic on the Post Road had come to a halt. The Mr. Bubble mess had finally grown so large it spilled over the fountain to the ground and then onto the street. It was then we realized perhaps we had used too much of the stuff.

We watched with utter glee as the commotion continued at 8:20. When the police and firemen arrived, even they had smiles on their faces. In the photograph on the front of the *Westport News* the next day, Mr. Melee stood beside the fountain with a wild-eyed madness and a broom, trying to push the Mr. Bubble blob out into the street. He was the embodiment of Jerry Lewis.

By 8:30 the excitement had died down, and it was getting dark. Shilling called his mom to come pick us up. She was not happy her son had been fired, but she did chuckle at the whole scene in front of the restaurant.

For weeks our escapade was fence-post news, and we relived and reenacted every moment of that night many times. And we all kept silent. No one ever knew who had created the "Great Blob of '72," as the newspaper called it.

A band of brothers were we.

She (Part 3)

HIRLINGTON'S PHARMACY WAS ON A corner of the Post Road. Truthfully, it was nothing special, and a few days a month, Hurl and I would help the old man move boxes in the back room. The upside was that we got to see the new shipments and discovered new products, candy, and stuff we didn't even know existed.

Occasionally we'd get a box of tampons, and that was fun. Once we played truth or dare to see who would open the tampon package and hold its contents. Of course we had seen the boxes in our moms' bathrooms, but we had never gazed at one up close.

I pointed to my crotch, "It goes in there? I mean, all the way up there?" Hurl was confused.

I nodded. "Must hurt like crap."

Hurl added, "Then all the blood gets soaked up. It actually absorbs the blood like some sponge vampire."

"Hurl, quit it." I was feeling squeamish.

"Your mom uses it. Your teachers use it. And soon, when you are a man, I will tell you how to use it in your you-know-what." Hurl crudely pointed to his butt.

"Shut up, dingus." I threw a tampon at Hurl's head.

He caught it, and thus began the Tampon Variety Show. He used it as a mini baseball bat and pretended to hit a home run. He held it in the air like a spaceship: "This is X1 Vagina. Do you read me, Houston?"

I was laughing along with him until Mr. Hirlington walked in casually to look for something in his unorganized pile of boxes. He turned his head and saw his son pretending to smoke a tampon in his mouth like a cigar. "Just what do you think you are doing?" he asked in a less than amused tone.

Hurl sheepishly replied, "Just having a little fun, Dad."

"Those are not a joke," he said sternly, but of course Hurl and I knew differently. "Put the ladies' articles down, and get back to the boxes. Afterward, I need you to organize the shelves out in the store. People can't find anything."

Hurl and I groaned. We knew the task at hand. Mr. Hirlington kept his store much as he kept his lawn: messy. Shampoo bottles were mixed in with cologne. Beauty supplies were buried deep in candy boxes. It was a pharmaceutical nightmare. It was no wonder Mr. Hirlington's business was failing. Once he'd been the pride of the town—the only pharmacy for miles. It was always crowded, and three people had worked for him—one girl just to mind the cash register. I remember him talking at dinner once about the possibility of opening an old-fashioned soda fountain. "You know, get the kids in the store. We got all the adults we can handle."

"That would be great," Mrs. Hirlington said in a funny way, like she was answering but not listening.

Unfortunately, no soda fountain would ever open. And Mr. Hirlington had to let his employees go one by one as the competition started to take away his once-thriving monopoly. The large supermarkets were getting wise. They began to offer an aisle of sundries. More sophisticated drugstores popped up along the Post Road, and fewer and fewer of Mr. Hirlington's faithful customers would show up. In fact, now the store was filled with elderly people who didn't know where else to go.

Hurl told me his father had received plenty of offers to sell his property or move his business into Stop and Shop down the street, but he wouldn't bite; nor would he work for anyone else in his life. He said he'd done enough of that when he was in his thirties and forties.

But Hirlington's Pharmacy was in trouble. Even a ten-year-old boy could see that. I felt bad for Mr. Hirlington. I felt even worse for Hurl. Having to watch his dad get crushed must not have been easy.

We finished lining all the boxes up against the wall. A few of them had a Hershey's logo on the flap, and it took considerable inner strength not to rip them open and gorge ourselves, but that probably would have hurt Mr. Hirlington's bottom line even more.

We walked through the dingy swinging door of the back room into the shambles of Hirlington's Pharmacy. I don't think Mr. Hirlington even realized what a junk pile it was as he told us, "You can see, boys, a few things are out of place. I need you to arrange products in the same place. Shaving cream next to shaving cream. Soap next to soap."

"Yes, sir," I said to my friend's dad.

"I have a firm count of the candy bars, boys, so no sticky fingers."

"Yes, sir," we both said this time.

Finally a small smile broke the cement expression of seriousness on his face. "Afterward I'll take you both to Carvel."

That was the incentive we needed. Hurl I started with the toothpaste, which was mixed in with all the BAND-AIDs, crutches, and canes.

"You straighten out all this old-people stuff, and I'll take the toothpaste and make shelf space for all the teeth crud," Hurl barked.

I wasn't even listening because just then Mr. Praddleton, Mrs. Praddleton, Bobby, and Melissa walked in. She looked as cool as ever in jeans and a Converse All Star T-shirt that made her feminine looks even more enticing. Bobby was his usual annoying self, wearing a striped shirt, white shorts, tube socks, and the finest sports footery money could buy.

Mr. Praddleton looked like a giant Bobby. He was wearing one of those expensive shirts with the Polo guy on the pocket, a gold watch, and alligator shoes. It was obvious they were loaded. But he was smiling in a friendly way that Bobby never did. I suppose being the most prominent doctor in town, he had to have a becoming demeanor.

Mrs. Praddleton was a mystery. Like Melissa she was not white. She was exotic. And she was not as old as Mr. Praddleton. She looked twenty years younger. A total babe, we would say. She had long black hair tied back with a yellow polka-dot ribbon, and she was tan, skinny, and covered in expensive-looking jewelry. It didn't take a genius to figure out this was Mr. Praddleton's second go-round in married life.

As soon as they walked into the store, Bobby and Melissa broke into separate paths, as if they were embarrassed to be seen with their parents. Bobby headed to the candy aisle. Melissa headed down my aisle. She saw me and smiled. Her walk changed from a casual stroll to a model-like strut. I was in way over my head. Like fathoms over.

Melissa said as she sashayed, "Hello, Jimmy Foxton." She was like Steve McQueen's daughter. So cool. So confident as she circled me.

This must be what it really meant when we dared one another to jump over the Hirlingtons' ravine and said, "Nut up."

This was definitely nut-up time.

"Hey, it's the girl who likes monsters!" God, did that come out of my mouth? A decent opening line. A direct, somewhat cute aside that would never give away my Don Knotts persona.

"Ha. You remembered." She smiled again, but this time, it was inhumanly cuter than the last smile. She didn't have a long black dress, but I knew what the Hollies were singing about in the song *Long Cool Woman (in a Black Dress).*

I felt it was safe to proceed with the monster theme. "Did you see on Saturday..."

"*The Mummy's Hand*!" we both semishouted.

"Love it when he runs around crazy, choking everyone with those black eyes," she said. If Melissa knew I'd spent most of the film with my head in Tante's arms, this conversation would be over.

I was more than curious. "Where did you learn about monster movies? Nobody takes that stuff seriously."

"My brother." A wash of sadness came across that face.

"Your brother? Bobby?" I looked over the aisle and saw the little jerk combing his hair and trying on sunglasses.

"No, my brother Miguel in Buenos Aires. He was two years older than me. Died in a car crash with my dad."

I had no words for that.

"It's OK. Happened a long time ago," she continued, and her glow returned. "There was very little to do there but play football and watch TV. Miguel used to make me watch all those movies because he was scared to sit alone. I learned much of my English from Bela Lugosi."

I heard Mr. Praddleton finally get his turn in line to speak with Mr. Hirlington.

"A carton of Viceroys, please," Mr. Praddleton asked, a little embarrassed (being a doctor and all).

"Yes, sir, Dr. Praddleton," Mr. Hirlington replied dutifully.

I didn't have much time to make my move. "You maybe want to watch Creature Features next week? I think it's *The Crawling Eye*."

"Not sure if my mom would let me, but you can come with us to our beach tomorrow."

I was stunned. My chest puffed out. The redness from my face drained. This was Jimmy Foxton's moment in the spotlight. *Ladies and gentlemen, it's showtime.*

"Let me ask my parents," she said.

"OK."

Melissa ran over to Mr. and Mrs. Praddleton. They both leaned over as she spoke. Suddenly they pointed my way. I smiled and waved like a goon. Mr. Praddleton looked me up and down as if I were in a police lineup. I was dusty and dirty from moving boxes. I had on torn shorts, and my shoes were untied. The homeless kids in the movie *Oliver!* looked more dignified.

They continued their conversation as if there were a problem. *I didn't make the cut* was my first thought, and then the *I wasn't picked for the kickball team* feeling rushed over me. I turned my head in defeat and stacked the remaining walking canes in their correct bin. And then I felt a tap on my shoulder.

"Can you be ready by ten o'clock tomorrow morning?" said Melissa.

"Yeah, of course."

"Great. Where do you live?"

"Eleven West Ambler Road. Last house on the road."

"Great. Bring your bathing suit. The club will take care of everything else. See you tomorrow, Jimmy."

I tried my best cool face, but it just turned into a goofy smile. Thankfully she liked goofy smiles, because she giggled.

"C'mon, Melissa." Mr. Praddleton walked by with his carton of Viceroys. He gave me a courteous smile. So did Mrs. Praddleton. Bobby gave me the finger.

I'd nutted up good.

I was on the curb the next morning at nine thirty in my best cool yellow shorts, striped socks, and sneakers I'd washed last night. But no towel. She'd said the "club would take care of" it. What did that mean? What club? We were going to the beach.

Twenty minutes of useless pontification, sweating, and unconfident thoughts later, a fancy brown Cadillac came up our street and rounded the cul-de-sac. Mrs. Praddleton waved to me as they approached. Good sign. I waved back. She opened the door and moved up her seat. Melissa was smiling. Next to her Bobby wore a look of discomfort as he had to scoot over to make room for me.

Mr. Praddleton managed a grin as he looked over his shoulder. "Hello. Jim, is it?"

Melissa interrupted, "Dad, I told you ten times his name was Jim."

"Just being polite, Melissa," said Mr. Praddleton right back.

Melissa smiled, and we rode the rest of the way to "The Club" in silence, heading past the Post Road and down the connector toward the water and a town called Fairfield. It would have been impossible to say something across Bobby to Melissa that he wouldn't laugh at, so I kept to myself. The windows were open, and the late July air kept us all comfortable with the smell of the seashore and seafood restaurants.

We pulled up to the Fairfield Beach, Tennis, and Yacht Country Club. A man dressed in green and white stripes quickly opened our doors and escorted us all out of the car. We sauntered—I don't think the people at the country club ever walked, so we sauntered—to the front desk, where the Praddletons were greeted by name and given green and white fluffy towels that looked more comfortable than my bedspread.

The concierge looked at my skinny frame condescendingly. "And you are…?"

"Jimmy Fox…"

I could not even get the words out before Mr. Pradelton said, "He's with us today, Rico."

Rico smiled and pulled out a small metal box. He opened it and stamped my forearm puke yellow. I felt like a marked kid with lice at school. He gave me a towel, and sure enough it was more comfortable than my bedspread.

As Mr. Praddelton looked out over the spacious grounds and ocean, he yelled back to Rico, "We'll take cabana four."

Rico nodded like a trained dog and wrote something down in his ledger. We strolled past club members, many of whom were staring disapprovingly at my yellow spot.

Melissa noticed that I was a little uncomfortable. "Oh, it's OK. Look. Those two over there have yellow stamps too." She pointed out two other newbies.

The concept of jealousy had never been a part of my biological makeup until today. The moment Melissa walked into the bathing area with her bright sundress, all the boys were eyeing her like she was a frozen Snickers bar. Too bad—this was going to be *my* time with Melissa, *my* chance to show off my wit, charm, and considerable knowledge of the horror genre.

But I could see this was going to be like the water-balloon game at the carnival. Whoever had the hot hand was the one she was going to be with. So be it. I was feelin' lucky. At first.

The Praddletons and I each took a padded lounge chair and put our towels out to warm up in the sun. Then we all went to the changing rooms. When I returned, Melissa was lying down, wearing sunglasses and a bikini. She looked soft and curvy and actually had boobs. Girls in my grade didn't have boobs yet.

Mrs. Praddelton looked like Charo, the sex kitten my dad would laugh at on Johnny Carson.

Mom didn't think she was so funny.

Mrs. Praddleton wore a tiger-skin bikini, reminding me of the slave girl Nova in *Planet of the Apes*. I was sure that was why Mr. Praddeleton was smiling as he unfolded his *New York Times*.

"Hey, Dad, can we go catch some crabs?" Bobby asked, bubbling over with excitement.

Mr. Praddelton hadn't even reached column one. "Now?"

"Low tide, Dad."

"Yeah, OK. Be careful."

Bobby, Melissa, and I got up and put on our sneakers.

"Bring us back a few lobsters," said Mrs. Praddelton.

As I went by, I got a better glimpse of her figure. Whoa. Major wombo jambos.

One of the pleasures of living on the Long Island Sound is that the water is usually calm. The beach can get hot, but it is quite sandy, and this stretch was pristine. To our left was a jetty surrounded by tide pools. I had no idea what it was about tide pools, but I could spend a day with my brother looking at all the minnows and catching crabs and putting them in our buckets.

Sneakers were essential. The rocks were wet and slippery from the fresh seaweed that clung to the baby coral. If you slipped, you could say goodbye to a layer of skin on your knee.

Bobby had to make this un-fun immediately. "The one who catches the smallest crab is a dildo."

I had no idea what a dildo was but I knew it was something I did not want to be. Melissa was smiling, and I don't think she knew either. Didn't matter. The wind was blowing her hair just like we were in a commercial. She could have been advertising a liverwurst sandwich, and I would have bought it.

It was my destiny to show Bobby and Melissa who was boss out here. In the tide pools, I was king. Bobby was a fool to suggest a contest out here. Instantly I knew which pools would harvest the biggest crabs: the ones closest to the fresh water by the end of the jetty and the pools with the biggest rocks. These crabs fight for the rocks, and the big ones are usually out there. I skipped between the large stones as nimbly as possible and found the deepest pool. The minnows were two inches long. They were swimming frantically.

That meant they'd come from fresh seawater and weren't stuck back by the beach in a puddle filled with stagnant seawater.

There were two large rocks, and in my experience, the flat ones usually held the oceanic treasures below. I was wrong. The largest rock uncovered a gang of small hermit crabs, which are usually fun to pick up but certainly not whoppers. The second rock was much smaller and covered with green algae, making it much harder to turn over. It was very difficult to get a grip when the boulder was so slippery. Positioning and stance were critical. So were my hands. I'd had many an index finger cut up, only to be further brutalized by the sting of saltwater. I balanced myself, pushed the rock over, and there it was. Huge blue pincers immediately pointed skyward. All those little back legs were fast too. It was almost lost in the long seaweed before the rock even revealed daylight. I had to move with James Bondian agility.

The trick to catching one of these whoppers without getting bitten is the challenge. Using both hands, the left hand attacks from the front, and the crab assumes it's in for a head-on assault. Meanwhile, the right hand sneakily reaches behind and grabs it from the back, where no pincers can reach. Some of these crabs are downright smart and won't be fooled by this charade for a minute, but luckily for me, this one was dumb. I grabbed the rear of the beast and hoisted it out of the water, slightly disappointed because crabs look much bigger underwater. But this one was still fist size. A beauty. Bobby Praddelton wouldn't catch anything close to it.

I held it up in triumph for all to see.

Bobby was looking at me with a sinister grin. He wasn't even in the water or by the tide pools. He gave me a half-hearted fake clap and nodded toward the beach. There was Melissa surrounded by five boys, who, in my mind, were all much older and better-looking than I was. I was crushed. Another ruse from Bobby Praddleton to make me look like a "dildo." He had succeeded. I laid the crab down. It scooted under a rock, and I wanted to follow right behind him.

I walked back up the beach, passing Melissa and her throng of admirers. The cabana was cool. A fan was now set up in the back. Fruits and vegetables sat on a tray in the center of the tent. It was a ridiculously opulent setup that would have had Tante screaming. Bobby was nowhere to be found, and Mr. Praddleton was just getting up for his prelunch swim. I lay down in a huff. It did not go unnoticed by Mrs. Praddelton. She lifted her sunglasses and looked at me. "Melissa likes you," she said with a warm smile. "She never asks boys to come to the beach with her. As you can see, she is a magnet that attracts flies. Those boys down there—they are just flies. They come, and they go. Nothing lasting like a true friend."

That stung a little. Did she mean a true friend who would also occasionally kiss her on the lips?

She continued, "You like the monster movies like my Miguel."

"I am really sorry he died, Mrs. Praddleton."

She seemed to appreciate that. "He made me a nervous wreck," she said, laughing. "All the Frankenstein and all the Wolfman. Where is the math? The history? The English? But I saw the happiness in his and Melissa's faces. What's a mother to do?"

I had heard that speech before and smiled. My expression betrayed me.

"Ah, your parents say the same thing?"

"Yeah, they do," I lamented.

"My husband—my former husband—and Miguel were headed to the River Plate to see a football game. It started to rain, and the streets get very tricky. Next thing it's just Melissa and me. She is very important to you? Just be careful. You have a long life ahead of you. Many girls. Many women. You are a good-looking young man. You have brothers or sisters?"

"I have a brother, Jeremy. Also there's my mom, dad, and Tante."

"Who is a Tante? Your dog? Cat?"

I laughed at that one. "No, she's my grandma"

She laughed too. "Oh, I am sorry. You love this Tante very much. I can see it in your expression."

I smiled. All the while I was trying not to look down at her boobs. I was doing a good job, but my neck and eyes were beginning to hurt. Mrs. Praddelton looked down at Melissa, who was still covered in boys. "Why don't you go down there?"

"I guess so," I muttered, defeated.

"You know, sometimes it takes a lot of courage just to stand there and smile."

"You think so?"

"I know so." With that she put her glasses back on and lay down on her padded lounge. "That's how my husbands caught me."

I got off my butt and walked down to the intimidating crowd. Melissa introduced me. "Hey, guys, this is Jimmy, my friend."

The other boys turned to say hello as a courtesy for Melissa. They couldn't have cared less who or what I was. I put on the fake half-smile my mother had taught me once at a funeral for an unknown relative. How was I supposed to look. Frightened? Sad? Relieved? Mom had said to make a half-smile and pretend to be nice or just stand there. That way people know they can come up and talk to you. Or if you're listening to a really boring story about waxing cars like your uncle Butch likes to tell, a half smile at least says you're interested and not rude. I'd made it through the funeral and used the half-smile trick a lot since then. It worked.

I half-smiled as some Neanderthal named Thad told Melissa about his collection of Beach Boy records. His whole act was negated by his buck teeth and neck pimples. Melissa was also half-smiling. When he started on his Jan and Dean forty-fives, I knew this was my chance.

"Let's go swimming, Melissa," I proclaimed, not asked.

Melissa gladly accepted. The rest of the boys gave me a look that said *I can kick your ass.* Even though I was a foot shorter than any of them, I shot them an *I can kick your ass* face right back. Melissa started to run, and I chased after her.

A lifeguard blew his whistle. "No running in the beach area," he yelled.

No running at the beach? Wasn't that what a beach was for? Melissa slowed down, and I guessed the rule worked in my favor. She looked at me with that smile and momentarily put her head on my shoulder. Then she started to run into the ocean. The lifeguard blew his whistle and gave up. I followed Melissa into the water. It was cold, and we were waist-deep. She looked at me and said, "Thanks for getting me out of there. Sometimes older boys can be so boring."

I didn't quite know what to think about that. Was I going to grow into something boring? No matter. I was in the water with Melissa Praddelton, who was in a bikini. A sudden wave came up and almost knocked her over, but I grabbed her by the waist. Her skin felt so slippery and goose pimply I just wanted to hold her there all afternoon, and I think she knew that. Melissa straightened up and said thanks.

We splashed each other in the face and dunked our heads under the water.

"Marco Polo," she said.

"Sure, you first."

She closed her eyes. "Marco."

I was on her left and playing it very close. I wasn't a bad swimmer and had some skills. "Polo," I whispered.

Her face lit up. I was so close. She immediately turned left, and I went deep under and around her.

"Marco," she said again.

"Polo," I said right behind her. She spun around and missed me again. This time I went to her right, and I could tell she was peeking.

"Marco."

Before I could even finish saying, "Polo," she had tagged me on the arm.

"You cheated," I said.

"So? Your turn."

We did the Marco thing for a few rounds, and I was getting frustrated. I wasn't going to cheat, but I was sure going to get her. I was extending my arms everywhere, flailing like a kite in windless sky. I shouted, "Marco," and put my two hands out front, ready to pounce.

Melissa shouted back, "Polo." She was behind me.

I turned on a dime and lunged forward with my two hands outstretched. I was not going to be beaten today. I got her. I opened my eyes, and both my hands were cupped around her two considerably firm breasts. I immediately pulled them away and said, "Excuse me."

Melissa was not shocked; in fact, I think she took pleasure in it by the way she smiled. "C'mon…let's go in for lunch."

It was a miraculous moment. And technically I had gotten to second base a whole year before I got to first base.

The rest of the afternoon passed without incident. We had a fancy lunch. Mr. and Mrs. Praddelton got bored and wanted to leave around three. Melissa and I talked about our different schools; her home back in Buenos Aires; and her other friends, who were mostly boys. We loaded up the car and drove to West Ambler Road. My lobster-red skin now made my yellow stamp even more evident. Mr. and Mrs. Praddleton said goodbye. Bobby scowled, and Melissa said, “See ya,” and handed me a note. As their huge roaring Cadillac stormed down our quiet street, I opened the note.

It read 227–6149.

Tante's Message

I'd learned how to saunter at the club, so I sauntered confidently through the front door of our house with Melissa's telephone number in hand. The living room and kitchen were empty. The back porch was quiet. I headed for the hallway to our modest bedrooms. Both Mom and Dad were standing outside Tante's room, discussing something serious.

This was always the case when my parents whispered quietly. It was a trait my brother and I found amusing and always mimicked in our room at night for a good chuckle.

I would say in a low tone, "Hal, Jim has eaten all the Oreos."

You could barely hear Jeremy respond, "That's because Jim is a fat pig, dear."

Then I would bean him in the head with my pillow.

But this hushed session with Mom and Dad was different. I saw Mom wipe away a tear, and suddenly all my masculine bravado from spending the day with Melissa drained from my body. Something was wrong.

Mom turned her head and gazed at me. She tried unsuccessfully for an everything-is-OK smile.

"What's wrong with Tante?" I didn't even bother to ask anything else. I knew.

Dad was never delicate with anything, even when it came to his mom's illness. "Tante is sick, Jimmy."

"Well, I know she wasn't feeling good, but she was still pulling weeds yesterday. And she even watched a movie with us the other night. She's just getting a little older, that's all."

Mom broke it slowly. "Your grandmother has an illness in her body that is making her weak. Cancer."

I knew what cancer was. And I knew people died from it.

Mom went on, "She's had it for a while now. We didn't want to tell you until it was time. And it's also making her very sad. That's called depression."

I did not know what depression was.

Mom continued, "Both of these things will make Tante tired and want to sleep. She was outside today and fell down. We brought her to the doctor, and he gave her some pills to make her pain go away. She has to go for tests and stay in her room."

My dad chimed in, "Son, we don't know how long she can last this way. She could get better.

And she could not. It's up to the doctors now."

"And God," Mom added.

"Where's Jeremy?" I asked.

"We told him this morning. I think he's feeling a little sad too. He's taking a nap."

"Can I go in there and see her?"

Mom and Dad looked each other in the eye. Dad made the decision. "Ten minutes. She has to rest."

Mom hugged me, and Dad tussled my hair. I knew this was not easy for them either. But at that moment, my world suddenly was feeling a seismic shift. What was I going to do without Tante in my life? It didn't seem possible. I'd never even contemplated losing someone I loved until now. I felt punched in the stomach and wanted to cry, but I would do that later and alone. I twisted the doorknob and slowly entered the room, scared down to my Keds.

She looked dead. Her skin was gray, and her eyes were closed in a peaceful quietness that betrayed her existence before the sickness. She would never rest, take a nap, or sleep away a day.

She was supposed to outlive me.

Tante opened her eyes and lifted her head from the pillow. "Chim, you've come to see your lazy grandmother lying in bed all day like an old lady."

"You? Old? Never," I said, and I meant it.

"Your dad or mom explain why I am in bed?"

"Cancer." Like Dad, I didn't know how to be delicate at this moment either.

Tante looked over at her nightstand. "Chim, will you get me a glass of water over there?"

I dutifully picked up the glass and gave it to her. Her hands were shaking, and some of the water was dripping on the bed. I held her hand steady as she took a long gulp.

"That feels better, thank you."

I removed the glass from her hand and put it gently back on the nightstand. "Sure. Can I get you something else? One of your cookies?"

"I have no appetite even for one of those right now. But I will. I'll get better. It might take a while, the doctor said, but he doesn't know me. You do. And you know I will be shoveling the driveway with you by this winter. I just have to get rest. That's all. Nothing to worry about, no matter what anybody says—including your mom and dad. You know this, right?"

I nodded.

"I don't want you to be afraid. I know I look like your friend Boris Karloff right now, but that's only until they get this out of me."

"You mean an operation?"

"I'll be in the hospital for a few days. Probably in a week or two."

"What are they gonna do?"

"They have to remove the sickness. It's in my stomach. Just like a bad bellyache. They do it all the time." She paused for a second to catch her breath. "Your mom says you went to the beach today."

I offered up my first smile since entering the room.

"With a girl, no less?" Tante returned the smile.

"Her name is Melissa. I like her. You know, like one of the guys."

"Uh-huh."

"I do. It's not like we're boyfriend and girlfriend or anything."

"Is she pretty, Chim?"

"I guess so. She gave me her number."

Tante let out an audible gasp. "A girl would have never done that when I was her age."

"Times change, Tante."

"I guess they do. And you will too. You're gonna grow up to be a fine young man, Chim."

"And you'll be there."

"I will try. Chim, just remember three things."

I leaned in closer.

"Help others. Love others. And love yourself. That's it. That's what there is to life. I know—I've had eighty-nine years of it."

"What about things like money? Money can buy you stuff."

"I've never had a lot of money. But if you worship a piece of paper, then you worship a piece of paper. So be it. Those who do miss the point of life. If I did that, I'd be lying here regretting everything, because I would have done nothing. Help others. Love others. And love yourself." She took my hand. "You remember that, right?"

"I will."

"I'm tired now. Have to sleep a little. Just a little." And she closed her eyes.

The Revenge of Mrs. Munson

MRS. BEATRICE MUNSON HAD BEEN in fake mourning for a month since her husband, Herb, died on Memorial Day after choking on a hot dog. She stayed in the house that summer with Duke, and that was just all right with me. The details surrounding Herb's death were sketchy at best, anyway. It seems Mr. Biser, Mrs. Munson, and Mr. Munson were having a holiday barbecue out back by the pool, the same place where Jeremy and I had seen Mr. Biser "making love" to Mrs. Munson…though I wasn't sure *making love* was the right term, since there had been more language like "That feels sexy" than "I love you."

In any event, the police found Mr. Munson on the ground with half an Oscar Mayer wiener sticking out of his throat. Word was Mr. Munson had been digesting an entire hot dog like a sword swallower in the circus. Mrs. Munson said he'd been doing it as a gag, and it all went south very quickly. The man was seventy-six anyway, and I could think of worse ways to go—like choking on creamed spinach.

The cops dismissed it as an accident, and Mrs. Munson resumed her life as Lily Munster. No one else on the road seemed to care.

Hurl, Shilling, Jeremy, and I, however, knew differently. At the fence post, we spent much time speculating on her evil plan and how she and Biser had done it. Hurl said Mr. Biser had just grabbed him while Mrs. Munson forced the tubular sausage down his gullet. Shilling said Mrs. Munson first put rat poison on the meat so Mr. Munson would gag on that and not the hot dog itself. Jeremy just said the guy was an idiot, and it had happened the way everyone said it had.

But that summer, every time I rode by her house, I could see the curtains in the window move and feel her vengeful eyes watching me until I was out of sight. Other times she was openly in the living-room window and mouthing, "Hmmpprrh," behind the glass. She had plans for me.

I was sure of it.

But there were bigger things to be concerned about that summer. Like Melissa Praddleton. And Tante.

It was August, and it was hot. My mom suggested a walk down the street so I could talk about Tante and "get my feelings out." I moaned. No boy in his sane mind would want to be seen walking down the street with his mother. But this was Tante we were discussing. I did need to express my feelings to someone. And Mom looked like she needed to talk more than I did. I said yes and just took for granted that I would be known in the neighborhood as Nancy Boy for a few days.

Just before our stroll, I had to be covered with bug spray as if we lived in the jungles of Peru. Mom did the same to herself. "It's for your protection," she warned me.

"Mom, there aren't even any mosquitos out there anymore."

"What about wasps?" she said with a smile.

Touché, Mom.

We walked briskly down the stone pathway leading to the street. "How are you feeling about all this with Tante, Jimmy? I know these things can be very confusing for a young man."

"I'm OK, Mom," I lied.

"I don't think so. I see it in your behavior. Your father's too. We are all scared."

I pondered that for a moment. It was the first time in my life Mom had opened up to me like that. Then it just came out: "Is she going to die, Mom?"

We made it to the street and began to walk down the little hill toward the Munson house.

"I don't know," she said. "All we can do is pray."

I had heard this prayer line in church a million times. It really had worked only once for me. Two years earlier, on Christmas Eve, I'd gotten on my knees and asked for a Lionel Train set. The next morning? Voilà. It was right under the tree. On other occasions, like when I asked for the Oakland Raiders to win the Super Bowl, no go. When I asked for a snow day last year? No go. So this praying thing was puzzling.

"You will put Tante in your prayers, right?"

I was willing to try anything. "Right now?" I asked, confused.

Mom laughed for the first time since Tante was diagnosed with cancer. "No, silly. Tonight. Before you go to bed."

We kept getting closer to the Munsons' house. I was already on the lookout for the curtains to part in the living room, but instead the front door opened. My mom and I stared at the empty doorway, and then there she was, ugly as ever. Mrs. Beatrice Munson.

"Hello, Mrs. Foxton," Mrs. Munson said without a *Hmmpprrh.*

"Hi, Mrs. Munson," my mom replied, demonstrating clearly they were not on a first-name basis.

The old hag walked out with Duke on a leash. I hadn't seen Duke almost all summer, and he did not appear healthy. In fact, he looked destined for the pet graveyard any second.

"Hello, James," Mrs. Munson said, eyeballing me.

"Hello, Mrs. Munson," I said back to her, withholding disdain and distrust.

"Would it be OK to ask you a big favor?" she asked, looking at my mom.

"Of course," Mom said, but she sounded apprehensive.

"Well, since Herb passed, his sister has been asking me to visit, and I just didn't have it in me to go there and talk about my Herby."

Mom and I stood there, wondering where this was going.

"Well, I am just going overnight and was wondering if Jimmy here could stay at the house tonight and watch Duke. He gets so lonely. Of course I'll pay him. Ten dollars?"

My mom looked at me, and I did everything I could possibly do with my eyes to say "Dear God, no!"

"Well, that's very generous of you, Mrs. Munson. I'm sure Jimmy would be delighted. He could use the money to take out his new girlfriend." Mom smiled politely.

I wanted to kick her shin very hard.

"Oh, that's wonderful. Our house is, of course, very old and a little creaky, and we don't have a TV, but there are plenty of board games Jimmy can play with. I'm so happy." Mrs. Munson looked at me, almost sneering.

Mom smiled uncomfortably and put her arm around my shoulder. I was being thrown to the wolves.

"I'm leaving at eight and coming back early in the morning. Jimmy, will you be here at a quarter to eight tonight so I can show you around?"

I nodded, and Mrs. Munson walked back up the stairs to her house. Mom and I continued to walk down the street, talking about Tante and feelings of being scared. Yes, I was scared. Very scared.

I was going to spend the night in the haunted Munson house.

Alone.

Later on I put together a little survival kit, including a sleeping bag, a flashlight, a Swiss Army knife, and some Cheetos. Call it battle gear.

Everyone was in the kitchen eating, including a very weak-looking Tante.

"Well, I'm off," I announced.

My mom reassured me (not), "You are right across the street. If anything happens, just call or run over here."

Running to Mommy is not the way you fight the powers of darkness, I thought.

Jeremy was laughing, knowing full well my fear. "You can always call Josie and the Pussycats."

Even Dad giggled at that one.

"Boner," I said.

"Jimmy Foxton. At our dinner table, there is no such language as that."

I apologized. Tante barely even looked at me. Her eyes were glazed over, and she was in her robe. Basically, Tante was not there.

It was seven forty-five and time to go. I walked over to the Munsons' slowly, looking at the few lights that were on. From outside, the house already looked dark. And huge. My imagination started to engage with thoughts of dead things in the basement and vampire bats hanging upside down in the attic—even worse, what if I saw a pair of Mrs. Munson's underwear?

Now *that* would be horror.

I rang the doorbell, and the crone took her time getting to the door.

"Hello, Jimmy," she said.

I replied but also wondered if this was it. Was she going to confront me on what I had seen that fateful night earlier that spring?

"Come inside. Just a few things to show you." Her bag was packed and by the door. Duke must have been upstairs, already passed out for the evening. Good. Last thing I needed was a toothless hound making all this worse.

Mrs. Munson took me upstairs to her bedroom, where Duke was sprawled out on half of the bed—I assumed the half Mr. Munson used to sleep on. Mrs. Munson told me to come up once or twice and pet his back to reassure him someone was home. We walked down the dimly lit hall to the guest room.

"You can sleep in here or downstairs on the couch. Doesn't matter to me," Mrs. Munson said. On the walls were pictures of her and dead Herb everywhere. None of the photos looked especially creepy; it was just that there were fifty of them. It was a shrine to herself and a deceased man.

We finally got downstairs, and she took me through the bathroom, living room, and kitchen. On the kitchen table was a plate overflowing with chocolate-chip brownies. "Jimmy, I baked these for you. Help yourself. Honestly, I don't eat them, so if you don't finish tonight, make sure you bring them home." This time she managed a fraction of a grin.

I half smiled.

"OK, that's it. I guess I'll be off. And you'll be happy to know I found an old black-and-white TV in the basement. I put it in the living room. You'll have to play with the rabbit ears. Maybe use some tinfoil. I remember Herby getting some football games on there."

I was more than relieved. "Thank you, Mrs. Munson."

"You're welcome," she replied.

I was most pleased for a TV. That night at 11:30, *Dracula Has Risen from the Grave* with Christopher Lee would be on. And nobody did Dracula better than Christopher Lee with the bloodshot eyes and sharp fangs. As they say in sports, "he's the man."

Mrs. Munson grabbed her suitcase and headed for the door. "I've left the telephone number to my sister-in-law's house by the phone. And of course the fire and police numbers are there as well," she said.

I nodded dutifully.

And then, with a bang of the door and a click of a lock, she was gone. The house was silent except for the ominous ticking of the grandfather clock in the living room. That sound was going to be a problem. Tick. Tick. Tick.

I looked around and thought, *This isn't going to be so bad.*

My first task was to turn on the TV and see what channels the old set would get. Turns out quite a few. I could watch the same stuff we had at home, just on a smaller screen. The new *Sonny and Cher Comedy Hour* was on, but I couldn't quite make out all of Cher's skimpy outfits, skin, and boobs.

I dropped my survival gear on the couch and went into the kitchen for a brownie. After my first bite, I knew this deal wasn't going to be bad at all. Turns out the old hen could bake. Not quite Tante-level, but enough to keep a boy happy on sugar all night.

I unfurled my sleeping bag on the couch. No one wants to sit on old-lady furniture without protection. Hair. Dead skin. Drool. A million disgusting things could be on that couch. For all I knew, there could be a set of false teeth under me.

I settled in as Sonny was doing something unfunny. I got up to make the TV louder and drown out the grandfather clock's ticking. While I was up, why not grab another brownie? I actually started to enjoy this. *What was I so afraid of?* I wondered.

I might even take a dip in the pool later. This was Hugh Hefner stuff. Baby, I was in bachelor paradise—old, decrepit, retirement home–smell paradise, but it still kicked butt. By 8:30 all was well.

Then I heard "eeeeerrrreeeeeek."

Was that creaking in the attic? Wait, what? I couldn't deny my ears—I'd heard sounds from upstairs. Not walking. Or stomping. But subtle and eerie noises. *It was probably old wood*, I tried to tell myself. Why do you always hear creaking at night? Old houses must creak in the day. But you never hear it.

Anyway, who's kidding who? I knew there was a werewolf upstairs.

Sonny and Cher were finishing up with an epic version of "Let the Sunshine In" from *Hair*. It wasn't *Fifth Dimension* good, but it was a solid effort nonetheless. I guessed if you write a great song, the real test is that anybody can do it and not screw it up. Purposely my mind was wandering to avoid the inevitable of being eaten alive.

I had to go upstairs and check it out. It was either that or flee the house like Pippi Longstocking. I chose to grab my flashlight and turn on all the house lights. I also picked up another brownie—perhaps as a bargaining chip for the werewolf. I passed the TV, and *Hawaii Five-O* was already on.

At the top of the stairs on the left was the bathroom; on the right was the door to the bedroom.

I chose the right: Mrs. Munson's underwear and Tampax would undoubtedly be in the bathroom, and I'd pick the werewolf over those any day of the week.

I looked in the bedroom, and Duke was splayed on the bed. He gazed at me, his eyes shining like illuminated marbles. For a second I couldn't tell if they were his or old Herb's. I stood there adjusting my vision and saw Duke looking tired and a little mystified. I took an apprehensive step toward the bed. So far, so good. I held out half of a brownie, shaking.

"Hello, Duke, boy. Good boy." I was disguising my fear poorly.

Duke put his head down. After all the times he'd chased our car, growled at us, and almost bitten me, I felt sorry for the old beast. He wanted nothing of the brownie but did vocally appreciate the petting and rubbing of his ears. Perhaps after all this time we were friends. As I gave him a doggy massage, I shined the flashlight around the room. It was immaculate. No clothes strewn upon the floor. The closet door and cabinets all were closed tight. It occurred to me Herb had spent a lot of time in here. *If I were a ghost, I would haunt my room for sure*, I thought.

My stomach rumbled something fierce. I kept on petting Duke, but I was wincing. Something was not right. I didn't feel like throwing up. I put my hand on my forehead. It wasn't hot. Was this that appendix thing my friends had told me about? I'd heard you could die if they didn't cut it out. The rumbling came again, this time louder. And my knees grew weak. Clearly this was a bathroom situation now. I stopped rubbing Duke and even dropped my flashlight. I ran to the stairs and debated going down, but there wasn't time.

Hustling to the Munsons' private bathroom was of no concern now. I just needed to sit on the toilet before my pants and underwear were soiled. I entered the Pepto-Bismol pink bathroom and got on the toilet just in time. Thank goodness.

Five minutes later, physically and emotionally drained, I emptied the entire air freshener can and went back into the bedroom for my trusty flashlight. The attic was still creaking.

The cord to pull down the folding stairs was directly above me in the hallway. I pulled it, and the stairs came down as if they were oiled. I jumped out of the way. They hit the hallway floor with a loud thump. Duke let out a half-hearted bark from the other room. I climbed the stairs quickly—I'd learned from too many movies that the slow climb always spells doom. I scanned the attic, and it was practically empty except for a few boxes. It was also clean: no spiderwebs, mice, or werewolves.

Relieved, I backed down and hitched up the folding stairs. My stomach was still growling but not enough to stop me from eating another chocolate-chip brownie. I strolled confidently down the stairs, knowing I'd handled my manly duties like a pro. I was proud of myself. I'd faced fear right in the face. Like asking out Melissa Praddleton. It was strange, warm, and nice feeling. Usually I tended to believe all the mean kids at school who told me I was a dweeb. Maybe, perhaps, I wasn't.

I passed the TV again, and the *Hawaii Five-O* team was well into their new investigation. In the kitchen I opened the fridge for the first time—B-I-N-G-O. A full jug of milk. This would surely cure my stomach problems. A clean glass sat on the counter, and I filled it with cold, delicious milk. I swiped a napkin and two more brownies for the final purge. There were only three left.

I sat back down on the couch. What was next after *Hawaii Five-O*? Where was the TV guide?

There was no TV guide. There was barely a TV. My choices for literature were *Life*, *National Geographic*, and *Reader's Digest*. I was in Mrs. Munson's living room. What else would there be? Get up and change a lot of channels—that's all I had to do.

The milk went down smoothly. Just what I needed after my near-fatal accident upstairs. Time to sit back and…*rrrrrrrrowwwww*….my stomach rumbled again. *That was just an aftershock*, I thought. *More milk and brownies will do the trick. Perhaps a few handfuls of Cheetos will help too.* No time for pain—right now the gang in Honolulu was chasing a crazed kidnapper through the city streets.

Rrrrrrrrowwwwwww. This was not a good sound. Not at all. I shifted my position as if doing so would cure my ills. I began to get that bathroom urge again. I tried to ignore the feeling and crawled into my sleeping bag. The milk and brownies were now both digested. They just needed time to settle in. *Rrrrrrrrrrowwwww.*

Please no. I don't want to use a strange bathroom again—especially in emergency bowel-movement status. I rolled over on my belly and thought a little pressure would make it go away.

No such luck. I unzipped my sleeping bag and didn't even bring the flashlight. *Hold it in. Hold it in. Just make it to the bathroom.* I ran full speed, opened the downstairs bathroom door, flicked on the light, and opened the lid. I tore off my pants, sat down, and let 'er rip.

Across from me was a large mirror. And on that mirror, written in lipstick, was *NEVER SPY ON ME AGAIN!*

What? I must have looked at that sign for a half hour as I did my business. It began to sink in that this message was meant for me specifically. I had spied on Mrs. Munson, and I'd known she had plans to get me back. But this was diabolical. Was anyone with blue hair that clever? I finally got up and thought how brilliant this all was. Too small and embarrassing of a crime to report to Mom and Dad; besides, would they believe me? Yet it was large enough to cause me some serious discomfort without getting hurt. She must have planned this for months.

I left the stinky room and went back into the kitchen. I opened every drawer and cabinet, looking for clues. Nothing. I tried the refrigerator and the freezer. Zero. I took the remaining brownies and threw them away under the sink, and in the garbage can, there it was. A Duncan Hines brownie mix box. And three packets of something called Ex-Lax. The box claimed it was "for gentle, dependable relief overnight." The word that caught my eye was constipation. I had seen this package in Mom's bathroom, and it would occasionally be on top of Tante's dresser when she visited. I ran into the living room, looking for the dictionary; it was wedged between something called *Little Women* and *The Dollmaker*. I leafed through the pages.

Con-sti-pa-tion
A condition in which there is difficulty in emptying the bowels.

This stuff made you poop. I'd been had. I spent the rest of the night half-asleep and half on the toilet. At dawn the front door opened, and Mrs. Munson came in with a spring in her step. I noticed that her eyes darted immediately to the empty brownie tray on the kitchen table. Duke was so excited he wobbled down the stairs with a pathetic howl.

"Oooooh, how's my Dukesy?" she said like an infant talking to a doll.

"He's fine," I said groggily. I was not going to give her the satisfaction of knowing my inner pain.

"And you—I trust you slept soundly." She smiled.

"I did, thank you, Mrs. Munson."

"Well now, it seems I owe a certain someone ten dollars," she said, fumbling through her purse. She handed me the ten. I took it, and she held it as well. "We're even-steven now, am I correct?"

"Yes, ma'am."

"Excellent. You have a good day, Jimmy Foxton, and I sincerely hope you enjoyed my special brownies."

I turned to walk away and mumbled a few choice words that would have me grounded for a week. Behind me I heard the slam of the door.

I spent a good part of that day in the bathroom. I might have lost five pounds in twenty-four hours. My mom kept asking me if I felt sick or had the flu.

"Nah, it's all those Cheetos I ate last night."

"Serves you right," she said cruelly. "Well, tonight we're going to have chicken and cheese enchiladas."

I said, "Great," and went right back into the bathroom.

A Gathering at Dusk

THE FENCE POST WAS JUST not the same the next evening. All the elements were there: a pink sky at dusk, humid air with a slight breeze in from the north, dry grass for sitting, and four boys who loved nothing more than to be together. But there was a heaviness, and we all felt it in our guts. This might not be the laugh-fest it usually was before bedtime. Feelings had to be shared. Thoughts had to be exposed. Destinies were about to be unfurled.

Shilling was up first, thankfully with a few much-needed laughs. He started rambling about his brother's latest round of clownery, which involved a large hookah pipe he used for weed. Seems Mrs. Shilling had found it in the closet and asked Ty what the contraption was. In typical Ty fashion, he told her it was an octopus he was building for school.

First of all, high schoolers do not build octopus models. That is usually left to elementary schoolchildren, if even done at all. Secondly, after Mrs. Shilling pulled out the six-armed contraption, she inspected the charred bowl of marijuana atop the instrument. Ty's days of building supposed aquatic animals were over. So—basically—was the rest of August. He was grounded.

That was a great leadoff, and we all chuckled, but then came the silence.

"I think our Tante is really sick," I offered up.

Jeremy added, "Cancer. She might not make it."

"Don't say that," I scolded him.

"Well, it's true." Jeremy sat down and folded his arms over his knees.

"Gosh, I'm sorry. I didn't know," Shilling said. "I wish I had more funny stories to cheer you up," he added.

"Nobody knew. Until she came here at the beginning of the summer. It's very bad."

Hurl just sat there, not saying a word, which was unusual. It went silent again, almost as if any of us were afraid to talk.

Finally Hurl spoke up. "I'm sorry about Tante, guys."

We nodded thanks.

He then said, "I'm moving."

Shilling nearly fell off his perch on the fence post.

"My dad told me we are moving to the shores. Just me and him. Well, you know my parents had problems—especially you, Foxton. I don't need to explain any more of it." He wiped a tear from his left eye.

"When?" I posed the big question.

"Next week. Before school starts. We're going to be in different schools until high school. Sucks."

"Sucks ass," said Shilling.

"Sucks Mr. Biser's ass after he ate tacos," Jeremy added.

"Sucks Mr. Biser's ass after he ate tacos and ate Mrs. Munson's ex-lax brownies." I succeeded in getting a big laugh.

"You gonna tell anybody she did that to you?" Hurl asked.

"I'd tell my parents, the police, and the FBI. Child abuse." Shilling put in his two cents.

"Eh." I shook it off.

"Yeah, if she's fooling around with Mr. Biser, her life is much worse than any of ours," Jeremy said.

We went back to the news at hand.

"Well, like, what are you doing? Is a moving van coming?" Shilling asked Hurl.

"Yup. Next Sunday. Then we have a week. Then Labor Day. Then new school," Hurl figured.

That sounded like a fate worse than death to all of us. I wanted to hug the guy, but you just didn't do that back then—no matter the circumstances. Hugs were for grandmothers and Santa, and that was it. Plain and simple. But I did offer my hand, and he took it. "This place will never be the same without you."

"Oh man, I'll be back," Hurl lied. We'd actually never see him again in our lives after the following week.

Shilling proclaimed, "Well, it's just simple then—we gotta do something wicked next week."

Our eyes lit up temporarily. The last fling of summer. Something different...perhaps even dangerous?

"The Halloween gag?" Hurl offered up.

Shilling shot it down. "Too early."

I really don't remember who thought up the Halloween gag, but it was one of the best gatherings of the year. We would find cheap dime-store Halloween masks, grab our pillowcases, head to the streets surrounding West Ambler Road, and knock on doors a week before Halloween. "Trick or treat," we would all scream excitedly.

The person on the other side of the door would be confused. Usually, the response was, "I'm afraid you boys are a week early."

The con then would be for all of us to appear completely clueless and then disappointed. On some occasions Jeremy was even able to offer up tears. The person answering the door would either shut it, give us candy they had bought early, or hand over some cookies. It was a fifty-fifty call per house, but at the end of the night, we ended up with a bag full of goodies.

Hurl was still very quiet and trying to stick a blade of grass into one of the ant holes, but they were gone until next spring. We didn't know why they left every year or if they all died, but we would miss them. The fireflies were gone too.

"Egg houses," someone suggested.

"Make the biggest bike ramp ever."

Shilling put up his index finger like a teacher trying to quiet the class. "Bales Pond."

"Bales Pond?" Hurl scowled. "We go there all the time."

"But not at night. Not overnight. Camping. And swimming with who knows what's underneath us in the dark."

It took a minute to click in, but the response was enthusiastic.

"Jeremy and I have a tent," I offered.

"And my tent will fit both me and Shilling," said Hurl.

Shilling added, "We all have sleeping bags. I have a few Roman candles left from the Fourth of July."

Shilling warned, "This is gonna be dangerous. And yes, we are going to build the biggest ramp you ever saw. Right into the pond."

We all sat on that one for a moment. Bales Pond was a nearby watering hole that was parentally approved because so many kids went there over the summer. The water was warm but very mucky. The thought of jumping in with a bike was not an inviting one unless you were brave.

"We'll use Ty's bike. It's been sitting in the garage for years. No one ever uses it. It has gears. A good seat. Decent tires. It'll be balls-out."

Our faces lit up like a glow-in-the-dark monster model.

Hurl was probably the most excited. Anything to have a few hours of not thinking of the dread that would befall him. "When?"

I said, "Well, if you're leaving next Sunday, then I say Friday night."

"Friday night. No wussing out," Shilling added, making it impossible to bail.

I reminded the group from my recent experience to bring flashlights, matches, lots of soda, candy, and chips…and, of course, our best nudie mags. The group concurred.

This would be a night to remember. To remember Hurl most of all. If I lost him *and* Tante, there would be a hole in my soul that perhaps could never be filled. I knew Hurl was only going across town—worst case, I could give him a call.

But Tante was beginning to worry me more and more. I was no doctor. Or preacher. But there was something that I could do.

Had to be.

The Bales Pond Farewell

"Absolutely no way," Mom said to the idea of a camping trip. But moms are like government offices: if you keep asking, submitting forms, and being pleasant, soon they break down, knowing that to deny you is going to cause them further hassles and headaches. After two or three days of cajoling, tag teaming, and general promises that we would be safe and careful and could run to the nearest house if anything went wrong, she relented.

Immediately Jeremy and I started gathering supplies, mostly taking sweets and chips from the kitchen in small amounts so our mom and dad would not notice.

Once a day I would go into Tante's room, and we'd talk about stuff—mostly old movies, my feelings about school this year, and the improvement of my grades. She told me she was getting a little better but had no strength to do anything, much less get out of bed. I tried to cheer her up with the plans for our camping trip. She had one word for that: "Boyz." That was it. I reminded her she would be pretty bored if there were two girls here rather than Jeremy and me. That got a smile at least. One day I reenacted the entire sequence when the creature from the Black Lagoon's lair is invaded, and he gets angry and lights a boat on fire with a lantern. Jeremy told me I did a great creature impression with the long outstretched arms and monstrous groans. Occasionally, when no one was around, I would practice the imitation in my parents' bedroom mirror. I wasn't bad.

Neither Jeremy nor I saw much of Shilling up to the day of the trip. I think all of us were assigned chores that week for the privilege of going on an overnight campout. We figured Hurl was just dealing with his own world right now. He was probably packing up his room and had no idea which parent he would owe allegiance to or even live with long-term. Now it was his dad. Tomorrow it could be his mom and her new boyfriend in Fairfield. It must have been painful. We all wanted to make this special for Hurl.

Friday at 4:00 p.m. we gathered around the fence post with our gear, Mom, and Mrs. Shilling. Mrs. Hirlington was nowhere to be found. At least Hurl didn't have to suffer the humiliation of all the goodbye kisses and "be carefuls" from both mothers.

We strutted down the street as a team—a tightly knit unit carrying backpacks and other gear. Shilling walked his brother's rusted bicycle. As we got close to the bottom of the hill, I could see Mr. Biser mowing his lawn, which, come to think of it, was all I ever saw him do. He saw me as well. For a second he stopped mowing, grunting, and sweating, and our eyes found each other. He looked me up and down and started laughing. He knew exactly what Mrs. Munson had done to me that night. Mr. Biser could have planned it, for all I knew. After a brief spell of chuckling, that old crank Biser put his head back down and continued to cut the grass. Somehow I felt at peace about all this, as if we were finally even. If I was the center of their amusement, so be it. It was over.

At the end of West Ambler Road, we crossed Turkey Hill to Ascott Street. After two houses on the right, a well-worn trail led back into the woods. It was marked with an official sign that had a circle with a dog on the inside and a line through it. Next to that was another wooden sign with camping, cooking, and fire instructions—as if any sucker ever read that.

There was much anticipation and talking on the way there. Shilling took the lead while we followed, already starting to groan about the weight of the materials we'd brought. Especially Hurl, who had one of those old army tents made out of heavy cloth and a jug of lemonade to boot. He was going to be sore.

The trees started to thin out and there it was: Bale's Pond. It was not a huge body of water, by any means. Maybe a tenth of a mile in circumference. But to us it looked like an ocean. Who knew how many frogs, tadpoles, and fish were in there? There was also a legendary snapping turtle everybody claimed to have seen but that actually didn't exist—a tall tale to scare all who entered the water.

There wasn't a cloud in sight as the rays of the sun shone on the water. We ran to the campsite, which was on the trail about halfway down the pond.

As we passed a discarded woodpile, Shilling said, "There's wood for our bike ramp right there, boys."

We were too excited to even look. Windblown and wild-eyed, the four of us sprinted for a place to put our tents down. Shilling got on the crappy bike.

"Hey, not fair," we cried as he easily beat us for the best place for a tent.

A small hill provided a bird's-eye view of the whole pond and the fields that surrounded the park. Jeremy and I had to set up behind them, but it did not matter; there wasn't a bad spot to be had that day.

Shilling and Hurl began the heavy task of putting up the heavy canvas tent, which I think was really made for the army. It had a serial number spray-painted on both sides. It was going to be hot in there.

Meanwhile, Jeremy and I had one of those newfangled nylon tents with the flimsy poles. Our dad had bought it for us the year before to camp out on the back porch, which we did often. This was her first real test in the woods. She was assembled in three minutes. Jeremy and I sat down and laughed at the Abbott and Costello antics of Shilling and Hurl piecing together their abode for the evening. Tempers were starting to flare between them. Jeremy and I fell over and cackled.

"Well, help us out, dick wads," Shilling said.

"Total asswipes," Hurl added.

"Jeremy, would you like a refreshment?" I asked my brother as a dignified gentleman.

"Why, Jim, I would love a Coke."

I went into my backpack and poured four glasses of Coke. I gave one to Jeremy and brought the others over to Shilling and Hurl. Just like in the commercials, we all drank them down together. Afterward we put their tent up like pros.

The hard labor done, we sat there on the crest of the hill. It was a moment that only youth could provide. Before us lay an afternoon of fun and, beyond that, a lifetime to experience all we could get out of this world. Some of it would be dark, some would be clear, and perhaps once in a while, when we got really lucky, we'd experience true brightness.

But the task at hand was to build the great jump ramp. We scoured the land before us.

"We should put it right there." Hurl put his foot down as the official ramp foreman.

"Right. Less weeds. And that is the real deep part of the pond out there," Shilling concurred.

Jeremy sarcastically said, "Yeah, I don't want to ruin that beautiful bike."

Hurl announced, "The way I'm gonna build it, very few of us will have the cajones to even try it. See that hill over there?"

Behind us was a small trail in the woods that led up to who knew where. Once again, our master ramp planner said, "You jump-start up there—just like Knievel. You get up a lot of speed. Maybe even take a practice run or two. Then put the gear in high. Pedal like the devil and take off into the sky. It'll be beautiful. Anyone bring a camera?"

We all looked at one another.

"Crud. We should document this," Hurl said.

"So where are we gonna find this jump?" my practical brother questioned.

"Right behind that little bunch of trees, they are building a bathhouse, men's and women's toilets, and a gift shop. There's wood all over the place." Hurl was clearly the man for the job.

We were all indeed impressed. He'd put more thought into this than anybody. Another wave of *I'm gonna miss my friend* circulated through my body.

Jeremy said, "Let's arrange our tents first and get the sleeping bags in the right place and the soda and stuff in the coolest area."

"You do that," Shilling said. "We'll get the wood. Probably too heavy for you anyway. Just don't get the Roman candles wet."

"Duh, Shilling," Jeremy said, peeved.

The three of us walked over the hill like desperados. Immediately we saw a world of very dangerous possibilities: long pieces of plank wood. Bricks. Hammers. Nails. Everything one would need to hurt himself.

Hurl chose two ten-by-five-feet planks of sturdy plywood, probably used for a wall or something. We felt like thugs as we picked them up.

"Don't worry; we're returning everything," he assured us.

Shilling and I let out some relaxed air. The last thing we needed was a hassle with the cops.

"Shilling, Foxton, grab the sawhorse, and pick up one hammer and as many nails as you can fit in your pocket. Gentlemen, we are about to break Guinness records here."

The three of us gave it our best evil laugh. As we crested the hill, Hurl begged for Jeremy's help with the boards. They dragged them down to the water's edge. Shilling and I arrived with the sawhorse, hammer, and nails. Then Jeremy, Shilling, and I returned to our perch and admired the master as he worked. Hurl anchored the sawhorse along the water's edge in the bottom muck. He shook it pretty hard, and it didn't waver. He gave us a big thumbs-up. He took the long plywood and began to nail the ends to the wooden sawhorse. He must have hammered in twenty nails. Overkill, if you ask me.

"Safety first!" he yelled with pride.

The structure now was quite fearsome—a long ramp with four feet of height. A lot of speed would guarantee serious air. Hurl took the bike and walked it up the ramp. Halfway to the top, the boards bent like weeds in the wind. Hurl was confused but figured out a solution in seconds. He rolled the bike down to the pathway and ran over the hill to the construction site. He came back with four bricks, which he placed under the ramp. He waved us over, and we made several trips with bricks so the entire ramp now had a solid foundation. It was invincible.

But before our bike extravaganza, it was time to jump in the water. We ripped off our shirts, and the four of us jumped in with a splash. Sneakers, socks, and all. There were supposed to be sharp rocks and broken beer bottles on the bottom, but we all knew inside our footgear was for the legend of Snappy the Turtle.

Everyone took turns dunking poor Jeremy until I had to step in. Brotherly abuse can go only so far. Our other favorite trick was to go under and pinch someone's ankle as if they'd been bitten by the turtle. No one ever fell for that a second time. Still, it was a good gag. The water was perfect, cool, and surprisingly clean.

We were giving one another headlocks when Jeremy started pointing at the tent sites. We all turned and saw Bobby Praddleton and two of his junior goons inspecting our ramp. It was only a matter of time before they raided the tents. We swam as fast as we could to our area.

"Hey, Bobby. Leave that alone," I hollered.

"Not doing nothin'," he said, feigning ignorance.

The other two were just watching him, as they had all day, most likely. I'd figured out early there were three types of kids in the world: normal ones like us; bullies; and the bullies' lackeys, who were the lowest species of all. His stooges du jour were Blesmick and Carter, two fourth-grade idiots without a brain in their skull.

All four of us reached the shore and shooed Bobby Praddelton and his friends away from our masterpiece.

"This is public land, man; we can do and go wherever we want," said Blesmick.

"Not on the ramp we built," Shilling shot back.

"Have you done it yet?" asked Bobby.

"Nope. Just waiting for the right time."

"When's that, Fart Face?" said Carter, actually believing himself to be amusing.

"The four fart faces," Bobby Praddelton continued.

Hurl just laid it out: "Get out. It's four against three. And we have a hammer."

The other three backed up a foot when Hurl pulled the hammer from the bottom of the sawhorse.

"Let's have a contest. Or are you tools too scared?" Bobby boasted.

Shilling just rolled his eyes. "Just get out of here. He might have a hammer, but I got nails. I'll put one each up your nose, swear to God."

"Wait," I said.

All eyes were on me.

I looked Bobby in the eye. "Just you and me."

Bobby accepted proudly. "I'll kick your ass."

"Whoever goes farther wins. The other goes home to Mommy."

"OK, who goes first?" Bobby asked.

"We both do. We're gonna do it at the same time. That way we can really see who goes farther."

Bobby wasn't quite sure. "Is the ramp big enough? I mean, wide enough for two jumps?"

"You too scared?" I momentarily slipped to his level.

Hurl and Shilling were looking at me like I was nuts. But there was something different in my persona ever since Melissa gave me her phone number. Confidence? Foolishness? I don't know. But I was not going to submit to Bobby Praddleton's cruelty ever again.

A scream arose from the other side of the pond. It was Melissa, her two girlfriends, and three boys who looked like they were in eleventh grade. Bobby paid no notice and went over to inspect the ramp. He rode his bike to the top to make sure it was steady.

I, however, wasn't even paying attention to anything except Melissa and her friends. She glanced over, and I waved.

"Hey, Jimmy," she shouted. "What are all you guys doing?"

"Making a world-class jump," Hurl yelled back.

Melissa and her friends started to swim over to the ramp. This was now not going to be a test of courage but one of pressure. Melissa was not going to see me as a loser on my bike twice. The older boys got out of the water and smiled at us.

"You dudes got some balls. This is wicked," one of them muttered.

Shilling took credit where credit was not due. "Thanks, man."

"You try it yet?" said another older kid. "Hey, Melissa, you see what your brother is gonna do?"

Melissa cupped her hands for maximum sound. "You be careful, Bobby Praddelton. Mom and Dad will not be pleased if you get hurt. You be careful too, Jimmy."

All the boys looked at me when she said that. Yes indeed—mighty impressive to have a babe like that tell moi to be careful.

"You ready?" asked Bobby.

"I need to get ready," I said.

"Hurry up, dork," Bobby said.

Shilling, Hurl, Jeremy, and I went over to the tent. I put on my shirt and wiped off my slippery sneakers.

"Are you nuts?" Hurl asked me.

"He'll give you a cheap body blow or run you off the ramp," Jeremy said.

"I'm ready for that. Plus he's not thinking about other stuff." I smiled. I walked out of the tent and behind the tree where the bike was. I pulled it around front.

Bobby chuckled. "You riding that piece of crap?"

"Yeah, you riding that nice bike into the pond?"

Sudden confusion overtook his face, but it went right back to arrogance. "I'll just get a new one if anything goes wrong." Bobby dismounted, and we walked our bikes up the pathway.

I'd never even tried the ramp once.

Occasionally we would look behind us and see the pond and onlookers getting smaller and smaller. Neither Bobby nor I had anything to say to each other. It was a silent, tense walk. I was scared and trying to not show it. I assumed he was doing the same.

I stopped at a pretty steep angle. "This is good."

"Higher," Bobby said.

I nodded, and we went farther. Looking behind us now was a gulp-inducing affair. Sanity must have kicked on in Bobby's brain, because he stopped. We were almost to the top of the hill. I was never one to sweat a lot, even when we played baseball in ninety-five-degree heat, but I was dripping with perspiration. Slowly I turned my bike around to face the steep decline. He did the same.

"You sure you want to go this high?" I asked. "We haven't even tested it yet."

Bobby just looked at me. Didn't even give me the satisfaction of an answer. It was now-or-never time, and Melissa was waiting below, her hand over her eyebrows, shielding the sun. I looked up and was glad that at least the bright light would not be facing us. That was some comfort. We both inspected our bikes as if we knew what we were looking for. I was looking for something, any reason to call it off right now. My stomach was a bowl of butterflies.

Bobby and I got on the bikes. We looked down at the crowd below. This was going to be a show for the ages, regardless of the outcome.

Bobby looked at me—nervously, I might add—and said, "On three."

In unison we counted down, and we were off to who knew where? In the air? Dead? Impaled on a sawhorse because Hurl had messed it up? In seconds all these thoughts crossed my mind, and we weren't even halfway down the hill.

I could see everybody cheering us on. My eyes began to water because of the speed. The old rust bucket kept side by side with Bobby's bike. We didn't look at each other because there was no time. Both of us had to hit that ramp just right, or we would collide. Closer and closer. Faster and faster. Suddenly the wood ramp was right in front of my front tire. This was it.

Bobby Praddelton hit his brakes with all the might he could muster, as far as I could tell. I heard the squeal and the thud when he hit the ground. As for me, I climbed the ramp and took off like a rocket. I thought I heard cheers behind me, but it all happened so fast. I was already twenty feet in the air and still sailing. I dropped the bike between my legs into the water below so I wouldn't land on it. As soon as I did, I climbed even higher. *Could I possibly jump the entire pond?* I wondered, and then old gravity kicked in. It was right then and there I let out the "Woo hooo" of all "Woo hooos." It was loud, and it was proud.

I looked down for an instant and saw a large ominous shape just under the surface. It was huge.

Oval. The giant turtle? Suddenly the shadow disappeared as it sank into the abyss. I fell pretty quickly and hit the water feetfirst. It must have been quite the splash. And I went deep. My sneakers touched the muddy bottom, and I headed back up for air.

When I bounced from the depths, everyone was swimming toward me except Bobby. They were cheering. Even the older kids were being vocal about what they'd just witnessed. Hurl and Shilling got there first and gave me a rare hug. Then Jeremy. Then came a kiss on the cheek from Melissa. I'd say I had done all right.

They told me I had flown fifty feet in the air. My jump was more than a football field long. Within seconds the story had already reached maximum exaggeration level. I certainly wasn't going to say anything to contradict it.

After my quick victory celebration, we headed back to shore, where Bobby was sitting on the ground next to his dusty bike. He had two skinned knees, a skinned wrist, and a few cuts on his face—nothing major but enough to look like he'd gotten into a bad fight with someone. He wasn't crying, but he looked like he was about to.

Bobby mustered up a few words. "Nice jump, Foxton."

I said, "Thanks, Bobby. What happened?"

He looked around at everyone. Very easily he could have claimed something was wrong with his gears, wheels, or chains. Instead he just said, "I wussed out."

My respect for Bobby rose tenfold that instant. He stood up and grimaced. Small amounts of blood were flowing from his wounds. Bobby never cried. He just got on his bike and took off.

I never had a problem with Bobby Praddleton ever again.

His two stooges left, going the other way. They weren't even going to follow their leader anymore, now that he had "wussed out."

Melissa and her teenage beach party returned to the other side of the pond. She didn't say goodbye, but a small smile did the trick just the same.

Hurl, Shilling, and Jeremy sat down and wanted to hear exactly what had happened and what was going through my mind. They looked at me with different eyes that afternoon. And not a one of us ever took a jump off that ramp again.

I also never said a word about the real monster I think I saw.

Comes the Night

THE SUN SET IN A glorious fashion, and we made a campfire. We burned hot dogs to a crisp on sticks. No one had remembered to bring any condiments except Shilling, who'd brought three cans of Cheez Whiz. So we smothered the dogs in cheese sauce like dipped ice cream cones. Warm soda topped them off, along with a few of Tante's leftover cookies, a box of Oreos, and an old Marathon bar Jeremy had found in the tent. There were no ghost stories. We mostly talked about the "miracle jump" as it would forever be referred to as.

Jeremy went into the tent first, excusing himself as a young gentleman only to be met with words such as "geezer," "old fart," and "butt crack." A half hour later, no one could keep their eyes open, and everyone packed it in for the evening. Shilling put out the fire with a half bottle of leftover 7-UP.

The night settled in. It had been a long day. Hearts, souls, and bodies were exhausted.

Until I heard that first *drip.* Then *drip, drip, drip.* Without notice it became a downpour. Jeremy stumbled out of his dream, opened his eyes, and smiled. This was indeed cool. The rain was hitting our tent like a battering ram, but the old girl stood her ground, and we just sat back and enjoyed the deluge. For about five minutes.

Then came the unzipping of our front flap. Shilling and Hurl entered with an armful of soda and other chemically enhanced food products. They were soaked.

"Our tent leaked," said Shilling.

"It's cloth, so I guess it wasn't built for rain." Hurl was a little embarrassed.

"And yet it was made for war," Jeremy said.

We made room for all four of us in that little nylon enclosure for nine hours. We could all sit cross-legged in a circle, and that was about it. Unless we ran home, there would be no outstretched legs tonight.

"This is cool, right?" Shilling smiled.

I added, "Very cool. No one think about whimpering home."

"Any chips left?" Hurl asked.

Shilling looked at the bounty of bags in his hand. "Only Bugles."

"Ugh." Hurl was not pleased.

I pulled out my AM radio, and "Magic Carpet Ride" from Steppenwolf was playing. We started singing.

Close your eyes now…
Look inside now…
Let the sound…
Take you awaaaaaaay…

Hurl broke up the chorus. "Was it just me, or was there something between Foxton and Melissa?"

"Nah, she's too old for me," I lied.

"Oh, come on. She gave you a kiss," Jeremy said.

"And if you tell Mom or Dad, I will pummel you till the end of time." Every brother has a favorite torture for younger siblings. Mine was aptly named *the Pummel.* It was a simple, yet effective device of torture to get Jeremy to admit anything, lie to our parents, or just walk around the room like a chicken. I would force Jeremy onto his back and place a fist on his abdomen. Then I would apply force in any measure, for any length of time, to achieve the desired result. This meant no bruises. I could hold my fist there for minutes until he could no longer breathe. Big brothers get all the fun.

"I'm not saying anything to anybody." Jeremy cowered.

"Don't worry; I wouldn't pummel you anyway. You're getting too old. Fourth grade next year."

Hurl and Shilling raised their eyebrows.

"Fourth grade is when the chicks get boobs, and you should at least get to second base," Shilling counseled wisely. "Gentlemen, let me show you." He reached into his bag and pulled out the foldout from a *Playboy*. He grabbed one edge and let the other two pages hang. It was Miss February 1968. She was a sight to behold except there were two small holes where her considerable breasts ought to be. Shilling smiled and put the tips of his index and middle fingers into the holes, and they actually looked like breasts. He wiggled them around and said in a full-on girly voice, "Ooooh, touch me. Squeeze my melons."

We guffawed.

"A trick from Ty," he said.

We all took turns putting our fingers in the holes. Hurl stuck his fingers in way too deep, and it appeared as if Miss February had drooping old-lady breasts.

"Ugh," we said in unison.

It was time for more munchies even though our stomachs were full and feeling queasy from the sugar. There was an eerie quiet except for the rain still coming down by the buckets.

Then Hurl just let it out: "I'm OK with it."

We stopped chewing, drinking, and moving and just listened.

"My dad took me by the new house. It was pretty cool. My room is much bigger. More space for models and stuff. I could fit the whole Thunderbirds set on my windowsill. You should see it, Shilling. Also saw the new school. I guess it's cool as far as schools go. They have a much better field and basketball courts. I can also walk to a store to buy candy. No more riding on the Post Road. But it's not going to be the same."

He stopped for a moment as if to summon up the courage to finish his thoughts. "I won't have my friends. The fence post. Even old witch Munson. But my dad says I'll make new friends, and he'll drive me back here or us to the movies anytime I want."

We all felt his pain. Deeply. None of us had been there, but we could now fully imagine what it must be like to lose just about everything you had come to know.

The next morning inside the tent was a pile of bodies. Arms and legs were strewn everywhere.

Hurl had his feet in Jeremy's face. Shilling's head was on my butt. The rain had stopped, but I could still hear the dripping from the trees onto the nylon tent.

But after that day, Hurl was gone.

As it always goes, young friends lose touch when they lose proximity. By the end of the next school year, I had nearly forgotten him unless when we would tell stories about the wasps or the "miracle jump." Except for that, he was gone from our lives.

We weren't being jerks or uncaring friends. That is just the way things are when you're a kid.

She (Part 4)

Jeremy and I stumbled through our front door and threw the tent in the hall closet, knowing full well we'd be yelled at later. Didn't care. We needed sleep. We rushed to our room, passing by Tante, who was being tended to by a doctor, a nurse, Mom, and Dad. Tante smiled at me and gave me a thumbs-up, and that's all I needed to rest my head on my pillow. Jeremy was already asleep. We went at it for hours, and then I woke in a panic, turned to the clock, and saw that it was only noon. Hopping out of bed, I woke Jeremy, but he just mumbled and began snoring like one of the three pigs. The top drawer of my desk held the most valuable thing I owned in this world: Melissa's phone number.

With a peek out the door, I could feel the house was empty. I treaded softly toward the kitchen, right past the front closet door, which was open with our tent lying on the floor in a heap, a not-so-subtle message from the parents: *clean this up, or else.*

But they weren't around. Perhaps they were taking a walk? Out for lunch? Who cared? I had man business to take care of. The green wall phone was where I had historically made all my lucky calls. Once I'd been the hundredth caller in a radio contest and won a night of bowling. Once we were late to the movies, and I'd called to find out *Diamonds Are Forever* started at seven thirty and not seven. We'd made the movie.

And today I was gonna ask a pretty girl on my first date.

I dialed three numbers and hung up. What was I going to say? What do those older boys talk to her about? "Just be yourself," Tante always said. I dialed four numbers and hung up again.

But what if she thinks I'm a dork? Be myself then? That's not going to work. Dorks don't get dates with girls two years older than them. However, I did do the "miracle jump" right in front of her eyes. That ought to buy me some points in the cool department. Also got the kiss on the cheek. Now or never. I dialed all seven numbers and prayed Bobby didn't answer the phone.

"Hello," said Mrs. Praddleton.

Thank God.

"Is Melissa home? It's Jimmy Foxton."

"Jimmy. How are you?"

"Fine, ma'am."

"So good to hear. Hold on. Melissa. Melissa."

OK. NASA countdown. Here we go. I heard the sound of the phone switching hands.

Melissa was laughing at something else when she answered, "Hello?"

"Hi, Melissa. It's Jimmy Foxton."

"The daredevil," she said, and that was true in more ways than one right now.

I have always found that with girls and first-date calls, there is a relative lack of chitchat: Get to the point. Make the deal. Score. And get out. "Uh, *The Crawling Eye* is on Creature Features tonight. I don't know if you've ever seen it?"

"That's a new one," she said. She started laughing again as if someone in the room was cracking her up. It was uncomfortable. Of course my paranoia raised its ugly head, and I thought Bobby was doing something mean again. I heard whispering. More laughing.

I swallowed hard. "Well, I was wondering if you'd like to meet me on my bike, and maybe we could order a pizza and watch it at my house?" I realized I hadn't even asked permission to do this from my parents yet. But a date with a girl should get a green light immediately.

"Uh, yeah." Again she sounded distracted. More whispering and laughter. Then she added, "That sounds fun."

I let out a silent sigh of relief. "Well, we could meet in the Saint Luke's parking lot. The place where we first met. Remember?"

"Of course I do. What time?"

"Well, seven thirty? After the movie my dad can put your bike in the back of the car and drive you home."

"I have to ask my mom," she said. I heard the phone receiver being covered up by her hand and a conversation that was muted. It went on for longer than I would have liked it to. "OK, seven thirty?" she asked, taking her hand off the phone.

"OK, great. I guess I'll see you then. And be ready—this is a scary one."

"Sounds like a plan. See you, Jimmy."

I hung up the phone. I was now officially a man—a rather superhuman man, I might add. No kid in our grade went out with juniors. As a gesture of my testosterone-fueled mood, I went over to the closet and cleaned up the whole tent mess. Jeremy was just an innocent little kid. What are older and more experienced brothers for, anyway?

I sat by the door and waited for my parents to come home. An hour later they came back with a bag of medicine for Tante. It wasn't a small bag.

"Well, how was the trip?" Mom was genuinely curious, while Dad headed straight for his mother's room.

"It was OK, I guess. Kind of sad to see Hurl for the last time."

Mom made a sad face that was also genuine.

"Mom, there's this girl I am friends with. Just friends. Can she come over to watch *Creature Features*?"

"Sure," she said without batting an eye and walked into the kitchen.

Hours later, after a good shower, I was in my best jeans and shirt, which wasn't saying much. However, and this is a big however, my hair was actually combed. Before leaving I went in to see Tante. She was sleeping and making a wheezing sound that was deep and very loud. I was so excited for this night yet so worried about the one person who actually seemed to understand me and what it meant to grow up. It was a strange conflict in the pit of my stomach. I closed the door gently and made my way to the garage. My bike was up against the wall and filthy from the last ride. I picked up a rag in the corner of the garage and wiped her down till she shone. The door was open, so I got on the bike and headed toward Saint Luke's parking lot. I made sure I would be at least fifteen minutes early so I could scope out the scene to find a place where I could look at least relatively cool. There were still six cars in the Saint Luke's lot. I also discovered a nest of birds in the tree above me. Two young robins were squawking away at the mother bird, and it reminded me of home. There were large pot holes that I never spotted before near the parking spaces. Now there were only four cars in the lot.

Looking down the road both ways, I could not see Melissa. Perhaps she was walking. That would take longer for sure. I got off my bike and swiped the kickstand with my sneakers.

Inside one of the school rooms at Saint Luke's was a clock that we always would look at to make sure we were home for dinner on time. You had to climb over a bunch of prickly bushes to get a glimpse. Thankfully I was in long pants. Sometimes in shorts you could get some nasty thorn scratches. The clock read 7:40 p.m. Only ten minutes late. That's nothing. Sometimes Hurl or Shilling would be a half hour late for a bike ride. I gently climbed over the prickly foliage and wiped the needles off my jeans. This was par for the course, I thought to myself. Nothing's wrong.

It started to sprinkle, and I was glad the best place to look cool was under the bird's nest tree.

More cars went by. And more cars left the Saint Luke's parking lot. Only one remained, and I guessed it was the head of the church because it was the nicest car. Once more I looked down the road, and she wasn't there.

My heart began to sink. She must have forgotten? Maybe she thought I said eight o'clock? The thoughts fluttered through my head, and I was trying to think about other subjects. Seeing Mrs. Munson naked? The Toro mower? Attacked by wasps? Nothing was working.

The sky was getting darker, and the clouds rolled in. I felt the first of a few drops on the top of my head. Perhaps she wasn't coming. Maybe I was just a joke to her. It didn't make sense because she was so cool at the beach club. I tried to fight off these thoughts like a boxer in a ring.

My mind simply could not get around what was happening. I was being logical, but my emotions were slowly breaking down. I sat there for another five minutes and decided to brave the bushes again. It was 8:15 p.m.

I saw a Chevrolet Camaro pass by with a couple of old dudes giggling and passing what I thought was either a cigarette or a joint. It looked like a joint from the way they were holding it so preciously. In the front passenger seat was Melissa. She was giggling too. And thank the good Lord I was behind a tree, because no one saw me. Prayers did work.

And then again, sometimes not.

Melissa was never going to come.

She lied.

And the tears came just like the rain from above. It wasn't a bawling cry like when our dog Snoopy died a few years back. This was different. I didn't cry as hard, but somehow I felt the hurt much more. Was I not good enough? Too little and insignificant to take seriously? What an idiot I was. Did anyone else know? Would I be made fun of at school?

In the coming years, Bobby became a schoolmate of mine till we graduated. We never talked, but we would nod to each other when we passed in the hall.

By the time I was in tenth grade, Melissa Praddleton was gone to college somewhere in Oregon. I never found out why she did not show up. Why she never called. We never came face to face. It wasn't until years later that I had the courage to trust another girl again.

Shaking off all the water from my dripping head, I waited until there would be no crying when I got home. I would tell my parents we met up, had a Coke, but she had to go home early.

I got back on my bike, and I rode her home.

This was a setback for sure, but there was something much more important to attend to.

My Tante.

Nine Tana Leaves

THAT MORNING I AWOKE EARLY, not because I was having nightmares about being dumped in a most cruel fashion, but because evil witches were chasing me through the catacombs of a haunted inn. I've always felt like one gets nightmares anyway so why not watch horror movies? This one was from *Horror Hotel*. I'll take the witches over Melissa Praddleton any day.

But this nightmare also gave me an idea. An idea that was, frankly, pretty idiotic even for a ten- year-old, but if there was some truth to the legend, maybe I could save Tante.

It was breakfast time. I put on my corduroys and sweater for church even though it was eighty degrees. Honestly. Would God get that mad if I wore shorts? Jesus wore a comfortable robe. Did we not learn anything from the Bible? Mom was in a dress; Dad was in pajamas. It was preseason, and he and Mom had a deal that the Jets needed prayers too. Jeremy was already on his fifth pancake. The boy could outeat a horse.

Mom smiled at me. Dad smiled at me. Both in sympathy for my poorly disguised performance to bring Melissa home for our *Creature Features* movie date. Was it that obvious?

We left for the Protestant Community Church, and I sat through the first twenty minutes, which were torture. Stand up, sing, sit down, stand up, sing, repeat. Then we left for Sunday school, which was the place where I learned about right and wrong, honesty and lies, and that the Bible teaches us to love one another, but a lot of it was just stories and that maybe didn't happen but taught a valuable lesson. A whale swallowing Jonah. Really?

After our lessons I met Mom in the parking lot and asked her a question that just about put her on the floor of the station wagon.

"Hey, Mom, can you take me to the library?"

"In the summer?" she asked.

"I really need to look something up quickly. Twenty minutes tops. Please?"

"Well, your brother needs new sneakers, and Carrington Sports is next door. Twenty minutes."

I happily agreed.

Our new public library was actually a wonder. The old library was a chore. You would wander down long, dark prison aisles to find a Dr. Seuss book. The new building was clean. Everything seemed organized. It was bright. They even rented out sixteen-millimeter movies and projectors. One time I rented *Citizen Kane* and thought it was interesting. Strange camera angles. It even felt spooky in places. The *Laurel and Hardy Murder Mystery* was my favorite. At least once a month my brother and I would show it on our wall at home and laugh every time, especially when Laurel and Hardy went to bed in their haunted room.

The desk lady looked like she was born in this century too. No glasses or hearing aid.

"Do you have any books on ancient Egypt or mummies?" I inquired politely.

"Probably a lot," she said as she looked through the files behind her. "A whole bunch in aisle twenty-three—"

"Do you know where?" I said even before she could finish.

"On the left-hand side, middle of the aisle. Third shelf up."

"Thankyouverymuch," I said like Melee without a pause in between words.

Down the row there were a dozen books on ancient civilizations. I loaded up my arms with ones that didn't look like dictionaries and proceeded to the reading. What I was looking for was specific, and it was immediately important to find out the truth.

The Mummy's Hand was from Hollywood. I knew this. Actors were playing the monster, the high priests, and the archeologists, but I also know some of the legends in these movies were based on some sort of truth.

Turns out:

There was a princess Anaka.
There is a temple of Karnak.
There are Egyptian tombs.
There are mummies.

Therefore, there must be something, maybe everything, to the legend of the nine Tana leaves breathing life into a person who was not dead but immobile. It was worth a try, and my emotions shifted significantly.

I could live without Melissa Praddelton.

Not without Tante.

Job one was complete now. I had to find a store that sold exotic plants and find myself tana leaves. I still had a few bucks from Mrs. Munson's overnight poopathon.

Mom always said something good comes from something bad. In this case, she was right. With geometry in school, I wasn't so sure.

I met Mom and Jeremy in the shoe store. He was trying on some new Pumas that almost had me raging with jealousy, but I didn't worry about that right now. I had to find plants.

"Mom, where can I find plants? Rare ones?"

Again she was taken aback. Perhaps even a little horror on her face.

"Jimmy, is this for that girl?"

"No. It's for Tante."

"That's such a nice thought. But we can get a bouquet at any flower store."

Had to be quick here, or I'd lose the sale. Think. Think. Think.

"Well, there's this plant that Tante likes the smell. From Egypt. Clears her sinuses", I said. I'd rather get that than just ordinary flowers."

"There is a place in Fairfield. Beautiful orchids. Remember that store with the carnivorous plants you liked to watch?" She shook her head and made an "I don't understand you" face.

"Yes. Perfect."

"For Tante."

"For Tante," I replied.

She looked at my brother, who had finished up lacing his shoes.

"Those fit OK?"

He nodded after walking on them for five seconds. Mom paid the "outrageous price" of fourteen dollars and ninety-five cents. Jeremy carried the bag proudly out of the store. We sat in our car without seatbelts and headed to Fairfield.

The Simmons Specialty Flower and Boutique was off the beaten path. In fact, it was in an upscale neighborhood that didn't seem to have any other stores. There was a nice-looking place with vines all over it, and a big greenhouse next door. Jeremy stayed in the car to worship his new sneakers. Mom walked up the steps and knocked twice. An older woman, Mrs. Munson old, opened the door, and she had a kerchief on. It was easy to see she had no hair, and the kerchief was covering that up. Must have lost it to age or some kind of sickness I didn't know. Kinda weirded me out and made me feel sorry for her.

"Welcome back." She obviously remembered my mom.

They hugged and whispered a few moments. I am assuming about the no-hair or sickness thing. Then the old woman turned to me.

"The one who is so curious about the *Nepenthes lowii*."

"What?" I was confounded.

"The plant that eats flies," she said mysteriously.

"Uh, yes. But this time all I need are tana leaves."

"Excuse me?" she asked.

"Tana leaves from the tana tree in Egypt. Thousands of years old."

She replied, "I have never heard of such a plant or tree. Let's look it up."

We entered the old house and took a sharp left to the hot greenhouse. It was sweat city in there. The lady pulled out a big old book and started going through the pages. First she looked at the *Ts* for *tana*. Then she went straight to Egypt and pointed a finger at a plant.

"I'm afraid there is no record of a tana tree. But there is a plant from Egypt that dates back to the pharaohs. A plant they used to worship."

I was all ears.

"It's still around and called a lotus flower."

"Do you have any?"

"In the back. They grow in water."

We passed by all the orchids, ficus trees, and flesh-eating plants to the back room where it was even steamier. In here, the plants seemed to be of another world. The colors and shapes were like nothing I had ever seen before. The lady went over to a water tank and gently picked up the stem of a most exotic flower.

"This is a lotus flower. It must be kept at a very high temperature and in water, or it will perish."

I began to count the leaves. One flower had six petals; the other had seven.

"I'll take nine leaves, please."

The older lady looked at me quizzically. "I am afraid we do not sell these by the leaf, or petals, as we call them. Tell me: what do you need them for?"

"They are for my Tante. She loves to look at them. Smell them. She is very sick."

This struck a chord with the woman, and she picked up two flowers without asking me anything more.

"I hope these give your Tante comfort," she said. "I know when I am not feeling well, all I have to do is come back here, and somehow my spirits are lifted." She smiled graciously at me.

We went to the front of the greenhouse where the cash register was, and she wrapped the flowers up in paper as carefully as if they were china dolls.

"For you. A gift," she said.

My mom interjected, "We can't do that. He has some money saved for this. What would be a fair price?"

"How much do you have, young man?"

"Eleven dollars." I was pulling out my wad of singles.

"Three dollars even, and we call it a deal."

Three bucks for flowers. What a gyp! I looked at Mom, and she nodded, so I paid the lady some of what I earned to sit on Mrs. Munson's toilet. But my task was done. I had the leaves, or at least it sounded like the same type of leaves worshipped by the gods of Karnak. It was ridiculous, I know. But so was my "miracle jump."

We got home just in time for Mom to start fixing dinner. Chicken dumplings. My least favorite of Mom's vast culinary creations. Tante had taught her how to bake. But dinners were a different story. Let's just leave it at that.

Dad was passed out on the couch in the middle of the Jets-Raiders game. I was so preoccupied I walked right by the TV, not even waiting to hear the score.

Jeremy ran to his room to put on the new Pumas and then try them out on the driveway basketball court.

I went to my room and closed the door. I put the wrapped flowers on my desk and cleared away all the paints, glue, and pieces to my Forgotten Prisoner of Castlemare model. It was basically a skeleton chained to a dungeon wall. Sounds dull, but if assembled and painted with skill and patience, it could replace the wolfman as the centerpiece to my collection.

I unwrapped the flowers with the utmost care. They were already a little misshapen and looked malnourished. This was good. If they dried out a little, perhaps they could burn easier. I took each flower and pulled off nine petals and put them in my top desk drawer. The rest were put in the bottom drawer just in case.

In our bathroom was a pile of old towels for spills. I wrapped the petals tight in the fabric, trying to squeeze every bit of moisture out of them.

Next I emptied my *Land of the Giants* wastepaper basket, for this was to be where the sacrificial leaves would burn and maybe, just maybe, awaken Tante. Even if it worked for a day, all would have been worth it.

The only thing left to do was set the clock for a quarter till midnight, for the ceremony had to be done at midnight. I had no rulebook. I don't know why midnight, but it just sounded appropriate for such a service.

I forced down a few chicken dumplings at dinner so as not to arouse suspicion. I excused myself from dinner. I went to the TV for the Sunday night double-header of *Mutual of Omaha's Wild Kingdom* followed by the *Wonderful World of Disney.*

After that both Jeremy and I were ordered off to bed.

Hours went by, and I never fell asleep. I kept thinking about my plan over and over in my head until it was perfect. Unfortunately, it did not start that way. The alarm clock, never went off and I sat up startled at 1:00 a.m. Jeremy woke up, and I eased him back down into a deep sleep.

I reached in the top drawer and took the leaves; they still felt a little fresh. I grabbed the trash can and a bottle of lighter fluid from my dad's wet bar. I was as silent as the night.

Opening Tante's door gave me an unexpected startle. She was gray and ashen as I have never seen before. I don't think I could have woken her up with a sudden noise even if I wanted to. I opened the window above her bed just a crack for the lotus-leaf formula to enter her chambers.

Leaving her room and heading outside, I banged my knee on the side of a coffee table, and it hurt a lot more than it sounded. I stood there biting my hand. Surely there would be a bruise the size of a banana there, and I would be grilled tomorrow as to where I got such a garish mark. No matter. The doors were unlocked as they were in those days, and I made my way to the window above Tante's headboard. Her lower room was ground level, so I put the can on the ground.

I counted out exactly nine lotus leaves and placed them in the bottom of the can. I tried to light them, but as expected, they were too fresh. So I poured the tiniest bit of fluid on top, and they flared up. For a few minutes I let them roast. Then I stirred the burned juices just like George Zucco and Edward Ciannelli from *The Mummy's Hand*. I wafted what little smoke there was toward Tante's open window with my hand.

I snuck back inside, careful to avoid the coffee table, and entered Tante's room. I closed the door tight so nobody could smell the unholy mixture floating in the room.

I waited.

And waited.

Until she finally opened her eyes and made a putrid face. "What is that smell?" she asked.

"Herbs and tonics to make you feel better."

"Smells like your mom's chicken dumplings, which I already suffered through earlier."

"Kinda."

"Chim." She looked at the late hour on her desk clock. "What are you doing here?"

"I am trying to make you better."

"I am getting better."

"But you don't look so good."

"Since when does an eighty-nine-year-old woman look good?"

"When you're raking leaves, or picking weeds, and making me do things I don't want to do, like plant seeds."

Tante was thinking.

"You know there comes a time when things must change, Chim."

"But not now, please, Tante. I need you."

"I need you too, but my body is having none of it."

"You can change that. The smoke woke you up, right? Take a deep breath of it."

"Anything but that."

"Please."

"Oh, OK," she said, slightly frustrated.

Tante closed her eyes and inhaled as much as she could. Afterward she made another face, indicating something smelled rank.

"OK, I did it," she said.

I got down on my knees just like I would to pray.

"Please. Please. Don't leave me. I know it sounds selfish, but I need you. I'm gonna need you. The whole family does."

"It's time."

"It's not time if you let the smoke work and put your mind to it."

She changed the subject. "I heard that girl was not nice to you the other night, your dad said."

"You see, that's exactly what I am talking about. How am I supposed to get through something like that without talking to you? I don't know what to do. All I did was cry. I still feel like, well, shit. Sorry."

"This is not a time to apologize. Besides, I have heard the word before."

My eyes were now watering. I was wondering if there was too much smoke.

"I will try, Chim."

"You have to do more than that. You have to promise me. For Jeremy. For Mom and Dad."

"How can I promise you something I have no control of, silly boy?"

I took her bony, frail hand, which just a month ago had at least had some flesh on it. There was a tear now flowing gently down my cheek.

"My heart hurts. For the girl who left me behind. For one of my best friends moving away. And for you. I don't know what to say except you are part of my life, a big part of guiding me on what to do. Mom and Dad don't do that like you do. Please."

"It is not me who you should be asking this."

"God?"

"God," she said.

"He never listens. Well, almost never."

"He's listening and watching right now. He sees what you are doing. Burning flowers in my window from some dumb mummy movie. Are those really tana leaves?"

I laughed. "No, lotus leaves. But they're from Egypt and thousands of years old."

"OK, He probably sees your effort. Now you must take that same exact effort and try to talk to Him. Not just ask for things but explain to Him your situation. Ask Him tough questions like why do people come and go in our short lives? Why did that girl treat you so rotten? You might not get the answer immediately, but you will get the answer. I promise you that."

"You see, how was I ever going to know stuff like that?"

I got up and put my arms around her. She tried to do the same, but it was painful for her. I could tell her face was wet with tears as well.

"Chim. Love others. And tonight you did that. Good boy," she continued. "I will try. I will not go out without fighting. I was about to. I am tired. But I see that I am still needed. Tana leaves? What a silly boy with a big heart."

We stayed like that for quite a while until Tante fell back asleep, and her arms fell by her side.

I wiped my face.

"I love you. I've never said that to anyone before. I love you," I whispered in her ear.

There was no expression in her face, but I knew she heard it.

I left, cleaned out the garbage pail, and went back to bed. Before I fell asleep, I asked God a lot of questions. Tough ones. And drifted off.

Two weeks later Tante went through her operation, and the doctor had said to us he'd caught most of the cancer in time.

"It was miraculous, really," he'd said. I wanted to tell him they should show mummy movies in his hospital because you could learn a lot, but I kept silent.

One month later Tante was in her car heading home.

And for the next ten summers, she came, and we did much landscaping, talking, laughing, and watching of old films.

When she finally went to God, she was ready.

And I was ready to say goodbye.

By that time I had a new girlfriend. Another house on another street. A bunch of new buddies. And even a new little brother.

My life on West Ambler Road had become much larger.

I was ready for the world.

I thought.

Ritual

"Brandy" HAD STOPPED PLAYING AN hour ago. I awoke and heard the sound of the needle scratching on the paper center of the record. I picked up the arm and placed the record back in its sleeve.

No more ghosts surrounded my car—only darkness and a sole figure looking out my old living-room window, most likely wondering who I was and about to call the police.

I wasn't welcome here anymore.

I turned off the record player and pushed the ignition button. Switching on the lights, I illuminated a place that no longer knew me. A bittersweet taste filled my mouth as my car drove slowly down the road one last time.

The next day I arrived at her gravesite. Jeremy was already waiting, garbage pail in hand.

In my satchel next to the Looking Glass single were three water lotus that had been wrapped in newspaper for six months. We put the leaves in the can and lit them on fire. The smoke wafted past black stains on the cold headstone—evidence of burning the leaves every year since 1985. As we watched the fire burn out and the smoke clear, Jeremy gave me a hug.

"I love you, man."

"You too, little brother."

"Your turn to take the trash can this year."

"Yeah, yeah, yeah." I complained. "You think this thing we do here every year keeps her spirit alive?"

"I do," Jeremy fumbled in his coat for his keys. "Didn't you ever see *The Mummy's Hand*?"

I chuckled. "Sometimes I think we just come here so we can have a few beers together once a year. Maybe I have forgotten?"

I picked up the garbage can, which was dented, worn, and now covered in rust.

"What's the first thing you think about driving away from this place?" he asked.

"Help others. Love others. Love yourself. That's all that matters."

Jeremy opened the door to his car. "See you at the bar. Your tab this year, bro."

I smiled, knowing full well my little brother was smarter than me in many ways.

We both drove off, leaving the graveyard as we found it—with immaculately cut grass, fresh flowers, and not a fallen leaf in sight.

We knew she'd like it here.

ABOUT THE AUTHOR

JAMES NOBLE WAS RAISED IN Westport, Connecticut. He is a copywriter and has written advertisements for Disney, Apple, George Lucas, Steven Spielberg, Tom Hanks, Ellen DeGeneres, and many other celebrities and accounts. Jim has won every advertising award there is and has shot commercials everywhere in the world. He lives in San Jose, CA with his wife, Cheryl, and a lazy cat named Cleo. He has a daughter, Rebecca, who is a screenwriter working in Hollywood, and a son, Oliver, who is a budding writer and graphic artist.

Made in the USA
Middletown, DE
26 May 2019